O Happy Day

THE HAPPY GOODMAN STORY

O Happy Day

by Jamie Buckingham

WORD BOOKS, Publisher
Waco, Texas

O Happy Day

Grateful acknowledgment is made to the following: Dodson Music Company, San Jose, California, for permission to reprint lyrics from "I Want to Stroll over Heaven with You," by Milton A. Dodson; Hemphill Music Company, Madison, Tennessee, for permission to reprint lyrics from "Thank God I'm Free" by James McFall; Jimmie Davis Music Company, Inc., Baton Rouge, Louisiana, for permission to reprint lyrics from "Come a Little Closer" by Rusty Goodman, "I Wouldn't Take Nothing for My Journey Now" by Rusty Goodman, and "Touch the Hand of the Lord" by Rusty Goodman; Journey Music Company, Madisonville, Kentucky, for permission to reprint lyrics from "Big Homecoming" by Sam Goodman, "Had It Not Been" by Rusty Goodman, "It'll All Be Over But the Shoutin'" by Rusty Goodman, "Most of All" by Bobby Goodman, "Who Am I?" by Rusty Goodman, and "Until You've Known" by Rusty Goodman; Rambo Music Company, Nashville, Tennessee, for permission to reprint lyrics from "The Holy Hills of Heaven" by Dottie Rambo; The Rodeheaver Company, Winona Lake, Indiana, for permission to reprint lyrics from "The Old Rugged Cross" by George Bennard; and Willis Publications, Inc., Farmington, Missouri, for permission to reprint lyrics from "I'm Nearer Home Than I Was Yesterday" by J. S. Eastman.

Library of Congress catalog card number: 76-144361
Printed in the United States of America

CONTENTS

PREFACE

I accepted the assignment to write the Goodmans' story with a certain skepticism over the genuineness of their happy, bouncing, handclapping type of Christianity. I could remember with vivid clarity the time, as a college student, I had wandered backstage at an all-night gospel concert in Macon, Georgia, and had seen some of the leading singers passing a bottle. Hypocrisy, I assumed, was just part of the role that gospel singers learned to play.

But such was not the case with the Goodman family. Even though I deliberately searched for it, all I found was a kind of holiness that permeated every facet of their lives—both on and off stage.

I traveled with them off and on for more than a year. The Silver Eagle, the huge, three-bedroom, fifty-five-thousand-dollar bus that carries the seven members of the family entourage, became my home, too, as I collected the information that has gone into this book. The Goodmans are acclaimed by experts as America's number one gospel singing group. They are on the road every Thursday, Friday, and Saturday of the year and are booked two years in advance. Their concerts carry them from the Mexican border to the cold climes of Canada, from the Atlantic to the Pacific.

JAMIE BUCKINGHAM

Part One
Follow the Eagle

On the Road

Madisonville is a sleepy little western Kentucky town of about twenty thousand. Not yet hit by the "shopping center splurge," most of the businesses are still clustered downtown near the square that surrounds the old, red brick Hopkins County Court House.

Most of the folks have lived here all their lives. That is, except the Happy Goodmans who are still considered newcomers by many of the old-timers even though they are Madisonville's most famous family. It is here that the Goodmans have built one of the most beautiful church auditoriums in the South, operate one of the largest mail-order businesses in the state, and have their own sophisticated recording studio.

It's early Thursday afternoon and business is slow. A few old-timers are sitting around the court house on the traditional wooden benches. Some are whittlin'. Some are chawin'. Some are talkin'. And some are just sittin'. Many of the shop owners have closed early to take advantage of the spring weather and "go fishing." But in the gravel parking lot of the old Life Temple at 35 Grapevine Road, next-door to the parsonage where Howard and Vestel Goodman live, things are beginning to happen. The old, white stucco building which once was the home of the Goodman church has now been transformed into an ultra-modern recording studio complete with thousands of dollars worth of electronic equipment. Below the studio is a suite of offices where young Roy Conley and his pretty wife, Loretta, handle most of the business administration of the Goodman enterprises, including Journey Publishing Company, which has

11

become a large business. Roy also serves as assistant pastor of
the New Life Temple and functions in all capacities alongside
Pastor Howard Goodman.

There is increased activity in the parking lot. The huge silver
and maroon bus, engine roaring at a fast idle, is being cooled
off under a drooping chinaberry tree. A garden hose runs from
Howard's house to a fixture at the rear of the bus as the water
tanks are filled. Sam and Bobby are loading clothes and equipment. Howard, Vestel, and Ricky emerge from the brick house
opposite the white studio building and climb aboard. Mama
Goodman, whose little trailer stands nearby, comes to the door
and waves good-by. It's almost time to go.

The bus is a modern miracle of transportation. Purchased
new from the Trailways Bus Company for sixty thousand
dollars, the Goodmans had it designed to suit their taste and
needs. It contains three double bedrooms in the back, a rest-
room, and four double seats up front for eight people. The front
seats are so designed that they can be turned toward each other
and folded down into two additional full-sized beds. As the
traveling motel for the better part of six families for three days
out of every week (sometimes more), it is one of the best in-
vestments any singing group has ever made.

On the dash of the bus, christened the Silver Eagle, lies a
beautiful black Bible, symbolic of the Goodman ministry. The
inscription on the flyleaf reads:

> This Bible is to ride on the dash of the Silver Eagle, a silent
> reminder that God rides every mile with those we love. There
> will never arise a problem but that the solution can be found
> herein. Drink from its fountain, it never runs dry. Lean upon it.
> It is always secure. Trust it completely, it will not fail.
>
> CONGRATULATIONS
> GRAMMY WINNERS
> THE HAPPY GOSPEL
> of the
> HAPPY GOODMANS
> Best Gospel Album—1968
>
> John and Linda Stalls
> Pentecostal Church of God

Bobby slips under the wheel of the huge house on wheels. The Goodmans are "in between" regular drivers and Sam, Rusty, and Bobby are sharing the driving duties until a new one can be found.

Howard and Vestel take seats directly behind the driver on the elevated platform of the double-decker bus. "Watch out, there," grins Sam who is just climbing aboard, "I don't know whether this machine can take all that weight over one wheel."

Howard hits his knee with one hand and laughs merrily. "Now boys, just don't worry about me or this bus. If something breaks down, we'll just pray and let the Lord carry us to where we're supposed to go."

Vestel looks at Sam and says, "Amen." Vestel's weight is an undetermined factor. However, between husband and wife there is reason to believe the scales would exceed five hundred pounds —and probably exceed it generously.

"Come on, Sam, get aboard," Bobby says. Bobby is given to few words, probably due to his background as a truck driver and roustabout, but one gets the impression he's not the kind to tangle with in a back alley.

Sam punches his little brother playfully on the arm and swings his legs through the door. Standing in the doorwell next to the driver he says, "Roll 'em, Bobby."

"Where's Rusty?" Howard asks.

"Isn't he asleep back there in his bunk?" Sam says, glancing over his shoulder and down the narrow hallway on the right side of the bus from which open three doors into the bedrooms.

"Better take a look," suggests Vestel. "No telling where he is."

Moments later Sam is back. "I don't see Rusty, but Ernie's back there sawing logs in the upper bunk." Ernie Maxwell, guitarist, is the only nonfamily member of the traveling group.

Bobby shakes his head impatiently and leans on the mighty air horn. The tremendous blast shakes the windows in the old church building and echoes across the south side of the little town.

"Bobby!" Vestel exclaims. "We're having enough trouble trying to get folks to like us. Blowing that train whistle ain't gonna make us any more popular."

Bobby grins impishly and pretends to blow a second blast when the door to the basement office flies open and Rusty leaps up the steps two at a time. Well built with curly hair and dark-rimmed glasses, he waves at the bus, stops to roll up the windows in his 1934 antique Chevrolet, and trots to the bus. He's carrying his brand new Gibson Super 400 guitar under his arm.

Bobby opens the door, and before Rusty can find a seat, the bus starts to roll. "Hey, watch it," Rusty shouts as he loses his balance, "I almost fell down."

"I just wanted to see if you were gonna protect your hide or that guitar," Bobby laughs.

Rusty, now firmly braced between the seats, grins and replies, "I could get a lot of hide replaced for what it would cost to re-place this guitar." Patting the guitar case, he continues, "Man, this baby cost more than a thousand bucks."

Rusty takes a seat across the aisle from Howard and Vestel. Ricky gets up from his seat behind his parents and opens the little pantry closet, digging out a box of crackers and some canned ham. "We've got a long way to go on this trip," Rusty warns, "you better not eat all that stuff up today."

Ricky grins and reaches over, slapping Rusty playfully on the head. "There's plenty here for everyone."

Rusty is right. There is a long trip ahead. First stop is the little town of Ridgeway, Illinois, just about seventy miles over the Ohio River to the north. From there they will turn the bus eastward across Illinois, Indiana, Kentucky, and into Welch, West Virginia. Friday night after the concert in Welch they will head south, crossing the steep Blue Ridge Mountains. Cut-ting through North Carolina and Tennessee, they will drop into south Georgia for a Saturday night concert in Douglas.

Douglas is a little farther south than the Goodmans like to travel on Saturday night because it makes it difficult to get back to Madisonville in time for church Sunday morning. By leaving immediately after the concert, though, the boys should be able to take turns driving and pull up in front of the church just in time for Howard to walk in for the 11:00 A.M. preaching service. The bus rolls slowly through the square in Madisonville. People on the streets turn and look. The Goodman bus is not an unusual sight, but it still evokes curious stares from the citizens. On board, the mood is jocular, informal, and carefree. Sam is still standing in the door well as the bus heads out across the countryside, and his natural humor and dry wit keep the rest of the family in stitches.

"Hey, look at that old hound," Sam says. "He's wallerin' on a dead bird." He points to a brown and white dog in front of an old farmhouse. The dog is on his side rolling over on the ground. "Purty soon he's gonna go in that house and you'll see everybody scatterin' out the back."

Howard laughs and joins in the conversation. "Let me tell you about that fishing trip last night. Old Rusty had that new Chrysler motor and I had that little electric eggbeater. Vestel and me cranked up and moved around the bend of the lake. Purty soon I heard old Rusty just a-crankin' . . . whirrr . . . whirrr. We pulled on down the lake and I heard him hollering. 'Hey, fat folks. Help!' We had to go back and pull 'em out to where the fish was biting. He never did get that high-priced motor to run."

Rusty grins and points out the window. "Man, look at that white German shepherd. That's the biggest dog I've ever seen."

"That ain't no dog," Sam retorts, "that's a pony." Turning to Bobby, Sam says, "I hope you don't get sleepy and let Rusty drive. As blind as he is, he'll kill us all."

Miraculously, the Goodmans have never had an accident in the Silver Eagle, although they have driven it more than one hundred thousand miles a year. "The Good Lord rides with us," Howard says.

The miles slip away as the bus leaves the settled communities and roars across the countryside. The ice chest at the front is packed with cold drinks, and occasionally one of the men will come forward and open one. Goodmans, it seems, are hungry all the time.

Ernie Maxwell has awakened and come forward. Picking up Rusty's Gibson Super 400, he picks out the haunting ballad, "Ever Gentle on My Mind." Next he props his knee against the back of the seat in front and plays the plaintive melody, "Tammy, Tammy, Tammy, My Love." The music seems to turn the Goodmans' minds to more serious things.

As the bus continues to roll through the southern Illinois countryside, Howard says, "You know, there is a matter we need to discuss. Our ministry is not exclusively in Madisonville. Sometimes we are required to be away from the church on Sunday, even though I don't like it."

Bobby enters into the conversation for the first time. "I think we're spending too much time away from our church."

Sam nods. "That's so, and we can't be away and expect the church to grow."

Howard counters by saying, "That's true. But still it's a big relief having Roy there to preach for me in case we get trapped and I can't get back. He has the same kind of burden for the church I have."

Rusty says thoughtfully, "Well, I'm praying that God will open doors, maybe through our new recording studio, so we don't have to be on the road so much."

"The church at Madisonville was ordained of God," Vestel says slowly. "But I don't think God would allow us to be gone as much as we are if we weren't blessing the people of America with our music. Besides, we're not just having 'church' in Madisonville. We're gonna have 'church' tonight in Ridgeway, and tomorrow night in West Virginia, and next month in Arizona. Every place we go we have 'church' when we meet in a concert. We ought to be praising the Lord for it."

"That's right," Rusty agrees. "Last week in De Ridder, Louisiana, I got my soul fed as much as in any Sunday service. Still, when I come home and Billie tells me what a great time they had in some church meeting, I long to be there."

"Vestel's right," Howard says. "God has given us this ministry and through it we are able to support not only ourselves but help support our church. At the same time we're being used to bless folks all over the nation. Let's just praise the Lord and do what He tells us to do."

"Well, now, that's settled," Bobby grins from the wheel, "can any of you tell me where we're supposed to go? We've arrived in the metropolis of Ridgeway."

Minutes later the air brakes hiss as the bus comes to a stop in front of the brown brick school building. It's 7:00 P.M. and the people are already streaming in from the parking lot. Bobby hits the door switch and the Goodmans pile out. The ride is over. It's time to sing.

RIDGEWAY, ILLINOIS

Ridgeway, Illinois, has a population of eleven hundred people. The promoter for the gospel concert, a middle-aged Nazarene woman preacher, meets the bus at the high-school gymnasium. "We've already sold twelve hundred and fifty tickets," she beams, "and we have another three hundred people on the waiting list."

"Praise the Lord," says Howard as he steps off the bus and shakes hands with the exuberant woman. "We'll sure try to give them their money's worth."

The school gym is three-fourths full although the concert doesn't begin until 8:00. Metal chairs cover the hardwood playing floor. Everyone is fanning. The sound of drums cascades from the stage as Ricky with sticks in hand takes a seat. Bobby and Rusty are setting up the sound system while Sam and Ernie work at the back of the gymnasium arranging their record and sheet music displays.

The crowd is warm and friendly and most of the people seem to know each other. Ridgeway has very few community attractions and people have come from many miles to attend.

Rusty has completed hooking up the sound system and moves from one mike to another testing. "One. Two. Three. Testing." The crowd grows quiet as his deep bass voice resounds off the walls. But the feeling of happiness, excitement, and friendliness still prevails.

Rusty moves to the piano and warms up his fingers. The stage

is becoming a mass of sound as Ernie plugs in his electric guitar
and tunes. The big loudspeakers are in place, and the smaller
monitor speakers, through which the Goodmans can hear themselves sing and so stay in tune, are ready. Sound is the secret. It
surrounds everything the Goodmans do. Across the nation singers
agree: if the Goodmans are going to be present, use their sound
system. It's the best.

Outside in the parking lot Howard and Vestel sit in the front
seats of the bus, resting. A crowd of fans has gathered around
the open door and some have even pushed up into the bus where
they are talking with Howard.

At 8:00 P.M. the lady preacher-promoter walks on the stage.
"What a joy to have you," she grins. She's wearing a black dress
with long sleeves, white lace cuffs, and white collar.

The first singing team are a man and wife who sing a couple
of old church favorites. They finish quickly and the lady
preacher is back on stage. "Did you enjoy 'em?" The audience
responds by applauding. "Now everyone scoot in so we can sit
the rest of the folks who're standing outside."

Next on the program are the Singing Henshaws and David
Overstreet. A baldheaded man and a lady with a guitar appear
on stage. They are accompanied by a good-looking, curly haired
man who takes his seat at the piano. It's the last time he is fully
planted on the piano bench though, for as his fingers hit the
keyboard, his feet begin to stomp and his backside bounces all
over the bench.

After a couple of songs the baldheaded singer motions for
applause as the bouncy piano player goes into a rapid arrangement of an old favorite whose melody is lost in the beat. The
audience picks up the tempo, clapping in time.

When they finish, the lady preacher is back. "Did you enjoy
'em?" There is more applause, led by the fat woman in the
sleeveless dress on the third row. "There's two chairs up here,"
the lady preacher says motioning toward the front as people
continue to crowd in the door. "We got folks standing. Come on
up, brother."

She looks around at the packed sea of faces before her and

says, "The local newspaperman is here, running around with his camera. Be sure you get a good seat and maybe you'll get your picture in the paper."

Next there is a poll of states and towns. "How many here from Indiana? Kentucky? Tennessee? Where you from brother? West Virginia! Give him a hand, folks. He drove all the way over here to hear the Happy Goodmans."

After encouraging those who are standing to find seats (there are none left), she says, "Now our top local talent. When I contacted them, they told me their finest dream was to one day sing onstage with the Goodmans. They could hardly believe their dream had come true."

The Clayton Trio—Bill, Delores, and their son, Scott—come on stage. They are obviously awed by the size of the crowd but sing a couple of numbers with good sound. Delores plays the accordion, and her son's voice blends well with the older adults. "I was just talking to Brother Goodman," Bill says, "and I told him, 'Brother Goodman, we sing a lot of your songs.' He put his arm around my shoulder and said, 'Son, just go ahead.' So we're gonna sing, 'I Wouldn't Take Nothin' for My Journey Now,' by Rusty Goodman."

As the trio exits, the crowd is on its feet, shouting and screaming, waving their hands, and stomping. Unannounced, the Goodmans have walked on stage. Vestel with handkerchief in her left hand. Big Howard at the piano. Bobby and Ernie on the electric guitars. Ricky at the drums, and Rusty and Sam before the mikes. They blast out with their opening number, "Happy Time."

As they finish, Howard pulls the mike over toward the piano bench and mops his brow, saying, "My, you folks have given us a *warm* reception tonight."

There is laughter mixed with more applause.

"Is it warm out there?" Howard shouts, waving one hand.

Shouts of "You bet," "Yes sir," and "Sure is," float to the stage.

"Well, keep those automatic fans a-going and we'll be ready to sing for you."

There is some side talk onstage and Sam breaks into laughter as Howard turns to the piano. His big fingers smash against the

keyboard. There is instant sound. Happy. Loud. Foot-tapping
sound. Rusty has picked up his guitar and is strumming on the
two and four beat while the other guitars hit the one and three
beat. The walls of the gymnasium act as sounding boards as the
Goodmans break into song.

The packed audience roars its approval. Whooping and
shouting they clamor for more. Above the din is heard Howard's
big voice, "Hallelujah! Amen!" The music picks up again.

The audience is at fever pitch. This is what they have been
waiting for. Every toe is tapping and every hand is clapping.

The applauding gradually subsides, and the strong, beautiful
sound of Ernie's lead guitar brings a subdued hush across the
crowd. Bobby's bass guitar backs him up and Ricky's drums are
soft as he uses the brushes. Howard's fingers, now gentle, caress
the keys as Vestel's full, rich voice, clear and beckoning, picks
up the lead. "The hills of home . . ." and the men join in, "are
calling me."

There is an audible sigh from the crowd as the music floats
into one of the most popular ballads on the gospel music circuit,
Dottie Rambo's "The Holy Hills of Heaven Call Me."

> The Holy hills of Heaven call me
> To mansions bright across the sea;
> Where loved ones wait and crowns are given
> The hills of home keep calling me.

The men join her as the music rises in intensity.

> This house of flesh is but a prison
> Bars of bone hold my soul
> But the doors of clay are gonna burst wide open
> When the angels set my spirit free.
> I'll take my flight like the mighty eagle,
> When the hills of home start calling me.

Howard turns to the audience as the song ends. "Isn't the
Lord gracious? He is wonderful! It's our great privilege to be
here tonight and sing for you. The people of southern Illinois

never fail to fill up the building when we come around. We love you for it. God bless you. And I hope you'll enjoy everything we do and everything we say."

He pauses, then continues with a smile. "The first thing in our lives is our work for Jesus. The Happy Goodmans have traveled many miles across the country. I remember my first revival meeting, September 9, 1939, down in Alabama. We've come a long way since then. We've seen times just like some of you have, when we didn't have anything to eat and no clothes to wear. But we always thanked God for what we did have."

Howard continues, "Brother Rusty was reminiscing one Sunday morning on these thoughts and the things that have happened in the lives of the Happy Goodmans, and he thought, 'If it hadn't been for Jesus, where would the Happy Goodmans be?' And he wrote down the words and music to what is one of his greatest songs. I want you to listen tonight as Rusty sings, 'Had It Not Been.' "

Rusty's deep baritone voice, acclaimed by many as one of the finest in the nation, comes through the speakers. The rest of the family join in on the chorus.

As the applause dies, Rusty turns to Howard and says, "I want to do another song. It wasn't supposed to be on the program, but I want to do it anyway."

Sam, standing on the far side of the stage, moans and looks at Rusty. "I figured you'd do something like that. The last time this happened you picked one none of us knew."

The music, like the stage chatter, is spontaneous. Seldom do the Goodmans sing a song the same way twice. Occasionally they'll even change the words in the middle of the song and there are constant instances of ad-libbing. Sometimes they stop and preach between verses. The audience is laughing at Sam's sad-faced remarks, but the fact is, Rusty has been known to pull out a song that no one else knows.

This time it is a new favorite, "Thank God, I Am Free, Free, Free."

Rusty and Sam begin to clap as Ernie's guitar picks up the lead. Almost instantly every hand in the room is clapping. Rusty

finishes the first stanza, and the instruments pick up the beat as
Vestel's strong voice takes over the lead.

"Whew!" Sam says as they finish and the clapping stops.
"One day I want Rusty to pick out a song that's not so high."

Rusty grins, adjusting the strap on his guitar. "Sam's supposed to be one of the highest singers in the business, but I guess
that one was too high."

"I wish you knew which key to put these things in," Sam
shouts.

"What key was it?" Rusty asks innocently.

"I don't know, but it shore wasn't right," Sam answers.

Howard interrupts, "You get four brothers and a sister-in-law
together and drop in my son and Brother Ernie and, man, we
have a time."

"Have a time" is a pretty accurate description for everything
the Goodmans do. Sam, who usually plays the straight man onstage with his poker-faced remarks, is the same way offstage.
His dry humor, sometimes bordering on what seems to be
grouchiness, is a constant source of laughter on the bus and at
home.

Howard continues, "Now, we're gonna let a guy sing who
seldom gets to sing. He'd prefer to stay in the background with
his bass guitar, but tonight we want him to sing. He's our youngest brother Bobby."

Bobby steps forward, unhooking his guitar. His melodious
voice picks up the strains:

> I want to stroll over heaven with you some glad day,
> When all our troubles and heartaches have vanished away,
> There we'll enjoy all the beauty where all things are new,
> I want to stroll over heaven with you.

Sam is back at the microphone. "One of the finest gentlemen
in the nation has just walked into the room. He's back there
standing against the wall. He's our good personal friend, the
Honorable Kenneth J. Gray, the congressman from this district."

The crowd turns and spots the handsome congressman who
waves in recognition. "Come on up here on the platform, Ken,"

Sam calls out. Congressman Gray makes his way through the crowd and takes a seat on the side of the platform. "He's the guy that sits up there and tells them how to spend our money," Sam says.

Howard interjects, "Boy, he sure is doing a good job of it."

There is warm applause and then Sam moves into his introduction routine of the family.

"Now everybody thinks that Vestel and Howard are our mama and daddy. I don't know why. I guess it's because they're so much . . . well, you know . . . just so much more." He holds his arms out in front of his stomach forming a circle. The audience roars. Howard and Vestel wait patiently as Sam continues his clowning. Sam then introduces the rest of the family and stops for a minute with Ricky.

"He's six feet two inches tall and weighs two hundred and thirty pounds—and he's nine years old." The crowd whoops with laughter and Sam corrects himself. "No, he's really seventeen, but the other night over in Indiana I said something about him being nine years old and it got real quiet. A little boy, way back in the building, said, 'Gollee!' "

Sam points to Howard. "We just got back from the beautiful state of California. I don't know whether you know it or not, but that is the land of the hippie. They raise 'em out there and ship 'em all over the world. And when we started back to the United States, we figured that every group ought to have a hippie. I mean you're 'in' if you have a hippie. So we got us one. I want you to meet him. Stand up, Howard."

The audience howls with laughter as Howard stands. Sam finishes in his deadpan manner. "That's our hippy-potamus brother. Make him welcome."

Howard takes over. "Now you can see why they call us the Happy Goodmans. We love Jesus and we like to have a happy time—all the time. We're gonna ask Sam to sing now, one of the great songs on the gospel circuit—one he wrote himself. It's called 'Big Homecoming.' "

As the tempo of the song increases, the audience comes to its feet. They are shouting and clapping. Backstage, in the wings, the other singers who were on the program earlier are on their feet. Their faces are beaming as they peer through the side curtains to get a better look at what is taking place on stage. Whatever else has happened tonight, it has been a happy night. There will be an intermission and then more music. The program will last until midnight.

The rest of the night and all tomorrow will be spent on the bus. No one thinks of that now, however, as the happy sounds of the Happy Goodmans echo through the night.

Welch, West Virginia

It's not all glory. Part of singing on the gospel circuit is just plain, hard work.

The Silver Eagle has been traveling since the early morning hours. It has crossed four states and is now entering Mullins, West Virginia, in the heart of the black-lung district. Here the roads are narrow, and the huge bus has to stop twice and back up to negotiate a sharp curve and cross a narrow steel bridge that spans the slag-polluted river running through the small community.

The rest of the miles are taken slowly as a combination of heavy rain and winding mountain roads force Sam, who is at the wheel, to cut his speed to a snail's pace.

The sky is clearing as they pull into Welch. The people come out of their houses and stand on the sidewalks. They wave enthusiastically as the silver and maroon bus rolls down the street. "The Goodmans!" a youngster shouts down the street. "The Goodmans are coming!" People run from their houses onto front porches to wave. Inside, Rusty, Ernie, Howard, and Vestel wave back. Ricky and Bobby are asleep in one of the rear bedrooms.

Sam wheels the bus into the parking lot behind the National Guard Armory. It is 7:00 P.M., only an hour before concert time. Now the heavy work begins. Crowds of fans and hopeful young gospel singers gather around the door of the bus. Rusty, a Tom Sawyer type in situations like this, gives them the thrill of a lifetime by *allowing* some of the young men the "honor" of carrying the boxes of records and sheet music into the armory.

Sam and Ernie are joined by Bobby, still rubbing his eyes from the nap. The heavy sound equipment is carried inside. Ricky appears in the door of the bus, scratching his head and buttoning his shirt. He will unload his drums and musical instruments. Each member of the family group has an assigned task and each does it quickly. There is no grumbling or questioning as they bend their backs to the task of setting up the stage and display counters.

A piano (specified in the contract and already tuned to A-440) is on the makeshift stage. Rusty walks by and shakes it with his hand, noticing as he does that the entire stage wobbles. Bobby grins, "If Howard hits that thing very hard, this place will really rock tonight."

Rusty goes to work with a soldering iron, mending broken speaker connections and taking a frayed wire off the monitor. Ricky finishes setting up his drums and turns to help Bobby with the big amplifiers. The two electric guitars are plugged in and tested, after which the Goodmans retire to the bus to dress.

Inside the bedrooms of the bus everything is as efficient as it was on stage. One man shaves while the other dresses. The top bunk has been folded against the wall giving more elbow room. Howard and Vestel occupy one room, Sam and Rusty another, and Ricky, Ernie, and Bobby have the larger room at the end. The blended smell of various shaving lotions fills the bus as the men finish dressing and take a last-minute stand before the mirror. Sam and Rusty take a swig from a bottle of cough syrup and shout for the others. It's time to begin.

The concert lasts two hours, and then the men pull off their coats and begin the work routine of dismantling the equipment and putting it back in the baggage compartments under the bus. It's hard work. Thankless work. They break down the equipment, unhook the mikes and amplifiers, wind up the hundreds of feet of wire, pack the sheet music, records, and tapes, and carry it all out to the bus. The heavier equipment is hauled on a hand cart which is the last thing loaded before the big doors

are slammed shut and the bus crawls out of the parking lot into
the night.

The ancient oaks, drooping with Spanish moss, line the
broad, straight avenues of Georgia's oldest city. The Silver Eagle
rolls past old Christ Church, first organized by George White-
field in 1740, five years after John and Charles Wesley arrived
in America as missionaries to the Indians.

Turning left onto tree-lined Victory Boulevard, the Silver
Eagle moves beneath the overhanging oaks while Spanish moss
brushes gently against the upper windshield. It's still early, but
the men want to get on out to the ball park where the concert
is to be held.

Grayson Stadium is the home of the Savannah baseball team.
At 6:15 P.M., however, the crowd forming is not coming for baseball, but for a gospel concert. Enthusiasm is hard to define, but
temperature is not. At least one thing is sure, it's going to be a
hot, sultry night.

The line-up of talent includes not only the Goodmans but
the LeFevres, the Oak Ridge Boys, the Thrasher Brothers, and a
local group known as the Butler Brothers. However, the man at
the gate, a personable young banker who moonlights for the
promoter on the nights of the gospel concerts, acknowledges that
it's the Goodmans who draw the crowd.

Situated between the pitcher's mound and home plate is a
huge platform mounted on the chassis of a house trailer. The
ends will swing out after the concert starts to allow for some air
circulation (which obviously is going to be needed tonight).
Powerful (and heat-producing) lights in the ceiling of the stage
beam against the floor. An additional platform extends outward,
doubling the size of the floor space.

The late afternoon sky is clear—at least, as clear as it ever is
in Savannah. The rank odor of the surrounding paper mills
hangs heavy in the air. Three mounted policemen with glistening white helmets roar up and dismount from their motorcycles.

They are the "outside" part of the contingent of six policemen (three will work inside the stadium) who will help handle the traffic for the evening.

The people streaming through the gates are a cross section of the Old South mixed with the new breed of youngsters. With the exception of a few singing "hopefuls" who are dressed in snappy suits and bright ties, there is a noticeable absence of coats and ties. The still night air is just too hot for "full dress." It's open-neck shirts and cotton dresses for most of them.

The smell of popcorn fills the concrete corridors under the grandstand. Three porters arrive carrying huge canvas bags full of crushed ice. The wind has died down, and there is a general feeling that the night will get even hotter.

The Silver Eagle slides through the narrow gate near third base. The other buses have already arrived and are lined up east of the dugout. Rusty, Sam, and Bobby get out to stretch their legs. Howard and Vestel, occupying front seats, look over the crowd in the stadium. Ricky and Ernie are dressing. The LeFevres have agreed to use their sound equipment tonight. After three days of taping television shows in Nashville, the Goodmans are relieved that they don't have to unload the heavy equipment from the bus.

The program begins promptly at 8:00. The Butler Brothers come to the stage and run through several songs and some light chatter. The crowd applauds politely.

The Oak Ridge Boys are next. Like the Butler Brothers they are a straight quartet, singing with piano accompaniment only. However, the magnetic crowd appeal is missing. Even though there is some applause, it is obvious that tonight is going to be a hard night to reach the people.

Something seems to be missing. Maybe it's the fact that the grandstand is fifty yards from the stage. Possibly it's the chicken-wire screen that separates the performers from the audience— placed there to catch foul balls. Whatever the reason, so far everyone is simply a spectator. Even those in the crowd that are clapping in time to the music seem detached and far removed from the action.

Willie Wynn, the high tenor of the Oak Ridge Boys, motions
for the crowd to clap. "Come on, help 'em out," he shouts and
motions with exaggerated clapping to get the crowd going. The
crowd listens—respectfully—but there is little life.

The Oak Ridge Boys introduce the LeFevres from Atlanta. The
LeFevres were the subject of a recent article in the *Atlanta Jour-
nal-Constitution Sunday Magazine* on the professionalism and
big business of gospel singing. This is "LeFevre Country," since
they are the only gospel singing group that has TV coverage in
Savannah. But even with that, there is a noticeable lack of crowd
enthusiasm.

Mylon LeFevre steps forward to sing a song of his own composition. It is a combination country-western-rock-gospel piece,
and the audience doesn't seem to understand. In fact, there is
little or no applause when he finishes. The people are sitting
deadpan. Like the other groups, the LeFevres are not making it.

The bright lights of the outfield pick up the fence signs in
center field. "Go Shopping Today . . . Liberty National Bank . . .
Savannah Sugar Refining Corporation Sweetens the South." The
signs seem to be getting more attention than the performers.

Mylon and Pierce LeFevre do an imitation of the Smothers
Brothers' comedy routine. Mylon plays the part of the stupid one.
There is a smattering of laughter from the crowd, and after one
more song the LeFevres leave the stage.

Enter the Thrasher Brothers. Dressed in Irish-green coats and
eggshell colored pants, they run on stage from the two back
doors, grabbing instruments as they come. One of them plays
the part of the smart aleck, grabbing the mike away from the
others and demanding all the attention. It's designed to get a
laugh, but tonight nothing seems very funny.

The Goodmans are next, occupying their usual feature spot
on the program. Sensing the lack of audience rapport, they
quickly take their places and open with "O Happy Day." But
the night is hot and sticky and the crowd is unresponsive. Even
Vestel's big, clear voice singing "The Hills of Home" doesn't
seem to stir the crowd, all of whom sit like mummies behind
the chicken wire. A sign behind home plate says, "No Pepper

Games Here." It's symbolic of what is happening this night in Savannah.

Intermission. Sam, his shirt soaked with sweat, shakes his head and remarks to Rusty, "Howard's not feeling well tonight. He even handled the introductions on stage like he wanted to get things over so he could get back to the bus. Things are dead, man, dead."

Rusty adds his opinion. "If I had my way, we'd never sing in another ball park. You just can't reach the people. They're too far away and the sound gets lost without a ceiling."

The Goodmans watch the second half of the program from the cool comfort of their bus. "Did 'ja see that?" Ernie asks in dismay from his vantage point in the door well. "The Oak Ridgers just sang a song and no one applauded. Look at 'em up there in the stands, just sittin' there."

"That's bad, boys," growls Howard. "But some nights are just like this. Those are good folks out there in the stands. They love gospel music or they wouldn't be here. But this just ain't the night—or the place. If we had that same crowd downtown in that old, hot auditorium, they'd be clapping and singing their heads off. But out here . . ." His voice trails off.

The long night is finally over and the Silver Eagle loaded.

"Looks like it's been a bad night all around," Sam says pessimistically as he strains over the steering wheel of the bus.

Vestel, who had been sitting quietly beside her husband, speaks up. "No, not quite. To me it was one of the most blessed evenings of my life."

"Blessed?" grins Rusty. "What could have been blessed about tonight?"

Vestel is serious. "During the intermission a young man came up to me as I was walking out of the grandstand. He said he had just returned from Vietnam where he had been badly wounded. He told me that while he was lying there on the ground, the blood pumping out of his body, that he saw my face before him. He said I came and stood beside him and sang 'Weapon of Prayer.' He said he felt the hand of the Lord on his body as I sang and the bleeding stopped."

The men on the bus have grown silent. "He told me he had bought our album 'Bigger 'N' Better' before he left for Vietnam. He played it over and over until he memorized every song. One of them was 'Weapon of Prayer.' When they got him back to the field hospital, the doctor took thirty-nine pieces of shrapnel out of his body and said it was a miracle he was still alive."

Vestel is sobbing now. "His beautiful young wife was with him. He had driven halfway across the state to attend this concert and tell me his story. He said, 'I'm here tonight because you sang that song.' "

There is a long pause. The only sound is the deep roar of the engine in the rear of the bus as Sam drives slowly down the moss-draped boulevard.

"You boys may have felt that tonight's program was a flop," Vestel says, "but to me it was one of the greatest blessings of my life."

DADE CITY, FLORIDA

This little Florida town that produces oranges, phosphate, Spanish moss, and mosquitoes is located in the center of the state about forty miles from the Gulf of Mexico. The Silver Eagle arrives two hours before concert time, having sloshed through torrents of rain in Georgia and north Florida. Dade City is dry, but from the looks of the sky the clouds could open up any minute.

"Better not spit out the window, Sam," Bobby chirps. "It'll rain for sure if you do."

At the main crossroads a white, fifty-five-gallon drum is perched under the traffic light. On top is a sign with a huge arrow: "Follow the Arrows to the Gospel Singing." The bus turns right and heads out Highway 52.

The parking lot at the brand new Pasco High School stadium is already half full of cars. Three other buses belonging to the Florida Boys, the Prophets, and the Singing Rambos are sitting beside the stadium.

The Goodmans park and start unloading. "Let's just stay close by in case we have to yank our stuff under cover," Sam mumbles as he glances at the swirling clouds overhead.

The grandstand on the west side of the field is jammed with eighteen hundred people. The speakers are set up on the platform which is located on the fifty-yard line. But there is a delay. A plug in one of the large speakers is shorted out. Bobby is on his knees in the wet grass working with a soldering iron. Something is needed to dry out the wet wires causing the short. Rusty whispers to Vestel who returns to the bus. Moments later she reappears with her hair dryer. Finally Rusty's deep voice comes through the speakers, "One. Two. Three. Testing."

The fading rays from the Florida sun reflect on the eastern clouds in brilliant hues of rose and purple. To the north the black clouds squat on the horizon. Maybe the rain will hold off, and it will be a nice night after all.

The master of ceremonies, dressed in a black suit, alligator shoes, electric-pink shirt, and white tie, calls for the crowd to stand for the invocation. A local preacher comes to the microphone. "I read somewhere that a man prayed and the Lord held back the rain three years and six months. I think a crowd like this should be able to hold it off for a few hours."

There is a titter of laughter that runs through the crowd. The preacher had accomplished what he came for—he'd gotten a laugh. He then calls for the people to bow their heads and in a loud, authoritative voice he calls for God to hold back the rain. His clever words draw smiles from the crowd—even during his prayer. He finishes with a pious "Amen." In the momentary silence that follows there is a reply: a low rumble of thunder in the northern sky.

The Florida Boys come to the platform. The crowd is responsive as Billy Todd thrills them with his deep voice in "Daddy Sang Bass." Tommy Atwood hits the high tenor notes and the crowd loves it.

There is still static from the mikes, but Rusty is working the control panel. He motions for Les Beasley, the lead singer for the Florida Boys, to change microphones. This done, the music continues almost uninterrupted.

The crowd gives them a loud ovation. Les Beasley makes his greetings. "Welcome folks. It's good to be here in Plant City." There is a moment of deathly silence and then a roar of laughter from the crowd. Les turns and looks at Derrell Stewert, the smiling piano player, and shrugs his shoulders. A foghorn voice from the grandstand bellows out, "Dade City." Les turns red and corrects himself, but the people love his mistake.

The black clouds have moved overhead. "If your license plate is 19-W-32700, you've got troubles," Les announces. "Your lights are on and your doors are locked." A fat woman and her little girl get up and waddle out of the stadium. They don't know it at the time, but their action is about to save them a lot of later misery.

The Florida Boys come on with a strong rendition of the comic spiritual "I Came Here to Stay." The many children in the audience are thrilled and excited over the funny rendition, especially Derrell Stewert's comical remarks and sounds. They give them a huge hand of applause.

The apprehension about the rain continues as Rusty and Sam stand behind the platform. Sam points at the dark line of clouds which now hover over the north end of the field. The overhead lights have been turned on and Rusty picks up one of the huge sheets of polyethylene which have been provided to cover the amplifiers.

The Florida Boys move into their third number, featuring Billy Todd. Just as they begin to sing "I crossed the hot burning desert," the first big drops of rain hit the concrete bleachers. People begin to fidget. Suddenly the lights of the field are filled with millions of sparkling raindrops, falling like silver dimes and quarters from heaven. The people are on their feet, and the Florida Boys, in the middle of a measure, stop and break for cover.

The two exit chutes or tunnels from the grandstand to the relative safety underneath are totally inadequate to handle the press of the crowd. Everyone is pushing and shoving trying to get to the concrete ramp underneath. Only about a third of them make it. The narrow tunnels are jammed like rivers filled with logs and the other twelve hundred people are left standing, unprotected, in the drenching rain. It is impossible to see across the field through the torrential cloudburst, and the grass is already several inches deep in water.

The Florida Boys, their black suits wringing wet, join with Sam, Bobby, and Rusty frantically pulling the musical instruments and expensive sound equipment under the platform—which fortunately is covered with artificial grass borrowed from a local funeral home. Ricky is trying to cover his drums with his suit coat and Rusty unplugs the echo plates and amplifiers. Les Beasley and Tommy Atwood are wrapping the studio piano with huge sheets of plastic polyethylene.

Bobby shouts at Sam, "I knew that cloud had something in it."

"Not any more," Sam grins, his suit drenched. "It's all down here."

In the tunnels the people are trying to shove those who have reached safety away from the exits. Having reached the dry haven under the stands, however, the people slow down or stop right in the doors. They stand—immovable—while the others still topside and soaked to the skin push in vain.

The rain is slackening. Some of the people, resigned to being soaked, turn and slosh back to their seats to recover pocketbooks, seat cushions, and other paraphernalia.

Suddenly it happens. Due to some oversight in construction, the contractor did not pitch the cracks that separate each tier of seats in the grandstand. As the stadium fills with rain, the water begins to pour through these cracks which are about ten inches apart. Almost immediately the haven under the stands becomes a shower room. A great cry goes up from the mob of people huddled below. There's no escape. The water is not dripping, it's pouring through the overhead cracks. It's like standing under a gutter spout in a hurricane, or in the shower with your clothes on. In fact, it is now raining harder under the stands than it was topside moments before. The people below turn and try to force their way back up the clogged steps to the safety of the open air, but the tunnels are still jammed with people.

The musicians are working furiously trying to get their equipment under cover. Howard, who had been tending the record and music stand by himself, quickly drags most of the sheet music into a small kitchen area that is protected by a ceiling. By now many of the record albums are soaked. Their cellophane covers will protect them but the pictures and sheet music take a heavy beating. Some are soaked beyond salvage.

Dottie Rambo turns to a spectator. "Last year we lost three thousand dollars worth of equipment in a rainstorm like this. None of us have any guarantee in our contracts which protects us from weather, and we can't carry insurance to cover such losses. We just have to take the loss and try to make it up later." She shakes her head and wades through the water in her stocking feet.

Outside on the field things are improving. The rain has stopped and the Florida Boys have come out from under the plywood platform. A Chevrolet van has been backed onto the playing field and Rusty, Sam, and Bobby begin loading the large speakers. The young promoter comes to the edge of the platform. His beautifully combed and sprayed hair is now hanging straight down the back of his neck. Wiping the water from his face, he turns to Rusty with a look of hopelessness. "You're not gonna leave, are you?" There is a note of desperation in his voice. "We couldn't help this, you know."

Rusty straightens up and looks at the young promoter. Everything in Rusty wants to cry out, "We're fed up, buddy, and we're going home." Instead he wipes the mixture of sweat and rain from his brow, gives a crooked grin, and says, "We'll do whatever you suggest."

"We told the folks if it rained we'd go to the old auditorium. It only holds twelve hundred and it's half a mile away. I doubt if more than a couple of hundred will try and make it, though. Everyone's soaked."

Sam walks up. "We want to do what's right. These folks paid good money to come out for the show, and we don't want to let them down. It'll just take us some time to move all this stuff up there and get set up."

"You guys got every reason in the world to be disgusted, but I sure appreciate your attitude. If the others will go with you, let's go on up to the auditorium and start over."

Rusty turns to the Florida Boys who have been joined by Buck Rambo. "You guys hear that?" Rusty questions.

"We heard it," says Les Beasley. "We're with you. Let's go." There is a long sigh of relief from the promoter, and he pulls off his coat and starts helping load the equipment in the back of the van.

The equipment loaded, Sam cranks up the bus and turns around in the nearly deserted parking lot. "Reckon anyone'll be up there at that old auditorium?" he asks.

"Look at that!" Ricky says excitedly, pointing through the windshield. "It's almost unbelievable." It seems that every car in the stadium parking lot is lined up on the highway that leads to the auditorium. The string of headlights seems endless.

Vestel shakes her head. "Would you believe those folks love gospel music? I think we're gonna have a bigger crowd in the auditorium than we had in the stadium."

Vestel's almost right. Fifteen hundred people jam the old building that has a capacity of twelve hundred. A large exhaust fan at the rear struggles vainly to expel the hot, steamy air. About three hundred people are standing around the walls. The rest are sitting on metal chairs, fanning and wringing out wet clothes. A cloud of steam is rising from their wet bodies and hovers around the naked light bulbs hanging from exposed rafters. Everyone is soaked, but they are ready for the concert, although it is now nearly ten o'clock.

The Florida Boys are still in good form and receive a tremendous ovation. Dottie Rambo's bouncy style thrills the audience and coupled with her strong southern accent makes her an immediate favorite. Her husband, Buck, and their daughter, Reba, join her, making an excellent singing team.

The Prophets are next on the stage. They go through several numbers and are enthusiastically received.

It is now 11:15 P.M. and the promoter is back onstage. "We proudly present the Happy Goodman family."

Dressed in mustard-brown suits, the Goodmans take the stage.

Howard had declared they'd not wear the brown suits on this tour again. But since the gray suits were drenched they had to shift back to brown.

After opening with "O Happy Day," Howard pulls the mike close to his face. "We're gonna do the best we can to sing for you and I'm sorry that you all got wet, but I don't think anyone got any wetter than I did."

Sam hollers, "That's just because there's so much more of you to get wet." The crowd shouts their approval.

Howard continues, "We're just like a bunch of chickens. Get our heads dry and we're all right."

The enthusiasm of the crowd is reflected in the Goodmans' performance. A crowd like this that would sit through a downpour and then come into a steaming hot building to hear gospel singing is the kind that brings out the best in any performer.

Sam is talking. "We've got a song written by a little preacher down in Louisiana. Occasionally folks ask where we get our music. Well, we get it from folks like this who send it to us. Sometimes they send us a tape recording, sometimes it's just the notes written on a sheet of paper. Many times we find a song that's good enough for us to record and publish. That's where this song came from. Listen while Brother Rusty sings "Thank God I'm Free.""

The audience reaction is fantastic. As the Goodmans sing through the chorus the third time, a woman in a blue and white striped dress stands up and begins waving her hands. The music from the stage gets louder and louder. Rusty finally pauses and says, "How dreadful it must be not to know Jesus. Isn't it wonderful that we can come out tonight and enjoy this freedom— freedom to worship, shout, and sing."

Rusty is moving into high gear with his preaching now. His guitar is still strung around his neck, but he's pulled the microphone close to his face. "Can you imagine blind Bartimeus sitting beside the road as the Master comes by, whispering, 'Master, don't pass me by'? No sir. Bartimeus was desperate. When he heard Jesus was passing by, he shouted. Then after Jesus healed him, he shouted some more. He could see the blue of the sky . . .

he could see the spectrum of the rainbow . . . he could see the
white clouds and the green trees . . . he could see the faces of his
loved ones . . . he could see Jesus. Now you try to tell a person
like that not to shout! I tell you, when once you were blind and
now you can see, brother, you'll shout. Listen, I want to sing it
one more time."

> Like a bird out of prison
> That's taken his flight
> Like a blind man that God
> Gave back his sight . . .

The music finally comes to a close, and Howard glances at a
big clock on the wall. "It's almost time for us to stop," he says.

"No, no," come shouts from the crowd. "If you fellows want
to keep on, just keep on," a man shouts. There is a roar of
applause.

Howard gives the cue and the group moves into "The Sweetest
Song I Know." The tempo increases and in moments Howard is
standing up. Leaving the piano bench, he takes the mike from
the stand and marches back and forth across the front of the
stage, singing with gusto.

> Amazing grace, how sweet the sound,
> The sweetest sound I know . . .

Howard moves back and forth across the stage, one hand in
the air and the other holding the portable mike. Never have the
Goodmans been in better form or has the music had a stronger
beat.

The hands of the clock read 12:30 as Howard finishes the
song. The Goodmans file from the stage, exhausted. It's time for
the intermission and the people make their way back to the
record counters and outside to catch a breath of fresh air.

Howard leaves the steaming hot building and wearily climbs
aboard the Silver Eagle. The engine has been left running and
the air conditioner has kept the bus cool. He collapses in a front
seat, breathing heavily. Moments later Vestel joins him. Lean-

ing over, she kisses him gently on the forehead. "You all right, honey?" she asks.

Howard sighs, "Yes, but Rusty sure did work me to death on that last number." Then reaching up and patting Vestel's hand he says, "But praise the Lord anyway, I'm thankful to be here." From the comments of those waiting for the intermission to be over and the music to start again—so are they.

Batesville, Arkansas

It is a hot, summer afternoon. The noise and activity of the county fair almost drowns out the shouting of the Goodman boys as they unload their sound equipment in the open-raftered building. The rough-hewn, wooden benches with straight, splintered backs seat about one thousand. The roof is corrugated tin with exposed two-by-sixes weathered with age. Brightly colored pennants hang from string tied to the creosoted poles that support the tin roof. The hard, dirt floor of the pavilion shows marks of having been freshly raked. Dusty, fine white gravel has been spread down the middle aisle.

Sam, Rusty, and Bobby are setting up the speakers. The stage is planked with sagging boards. The back wall, which is warped tongue-and-groove construction, shows faint evidences of having once been painted green. Exposed light bulbs hang from the rafters.

"Careful there, Ricky," shouts Bobby, "you'll get your hands sweaty carrying those drums."

Ricky grins, runs his fingers through his curly hair, and continues to set up his blue sparkle drum set. The Goodmans will just have time to run back to their motel room to change clothes before the concert begins.

The cheap sounds of the midway fill the air. The gaudy lights of the merry-go-round, the Ferris wheel, and the tilt-a-whirl dominate the night sky. Black power cables are everywhere across the sawdust-covered fairground. It hasn't rained in two months, and the powdery dust rises in little puffs with every step.

There is a noticeable absence of the regular carny and midway bawdiness. Not to be seen are the bingo games, pitching pennies, and bump-and-grind strippers. Such would be totally unacceptable in Batesville where fundamental Christianity has so far resisted the influences of the outside world.

It is 7:00 P.M. and the lady promoter comes to the microphone at the tabernacle. More than a thousand people have jammed under the roof, sitting on the hard benches. Another five or six hundred have crowded around the sides and back of the pavilion.

The Happy Goodmans are introduced and when Howard takes his seat at the piano, there is a smattering of applause. "You'll have to do better than that," he shouts into the microphone. "Are you glad to see the Happy Goodmans tonight?"

This time there is an enthusiastic roar and the Goodmans break into "We Are All So Happy." The crowd joins in clapping with them. The show is on.

They finish, and Sam turns away from the mike with his characteristic coughing, grinning at the people who are crowded against the side of the stage. They love his personal attention and clap loudly as the piano picks up the tempo and swings back into the theme song.

Then Ernie's guitar takes the lead on the plaintive strains of "The Hills of Home," and Vestel's big voice booms through the night.

Vestel picks up the melody as Howard murmurs into the microphone, "Sing it, honey." The crowd continues to grow larger as the people wander off the midway and stand in the shadows around the pavilion.

Howard's nimble fingers hammer the keys of the piano as the group starts singing, "Give Up, and Let Jesus Take Over."

When the music comes to a halt, Howard says, "We're glad to be here tonight. It may get a little bit louder because we've got to compete with the Ferris wheel."

Sam, joking, moves to the mike and says, "We're gonna have to sing louder than the Ferris wheel 'cause there's a few of us who sure can't ride it." He holds his arms in an exaggerated circle in front of his stomach and points at Howard's huge form draped across the chair at the piano. The crowd howls with laughter.

Howard glances over his shoulder at Sam with imitation disgust and says, "Well, speak for yourself, boy. I could ride it."

Howard shakes his head and pulls the mike back to his face. "My, this is a friendly bunch of people. How many of you have seen the Happy Goodmans on television?"

Almost every hand goes up. The people are leaning forward, grinning. A nice-looking woman in her forties is sitting on the front row next to a much older man. Their hands are clasped and eyes glittering. They've waited, perhaps even prayed, to see the Goodmans in person and are drinking in every word.

"Sam," Howard says, "tell the folks who we are."

Sam says, "How many of you were here last night to hear the Florida Boys?" Hands go up all over the house.

"Fine!" he continues. "Well, I'm gonna tell you right now. This is the greatest place in the world to come to." He pauses while the applause dies. "Probably because there ain't no place else to go in Batesville."

There is a roar of applause from the young people in particular. Many of the adults grin and nod their heads. "You probably couldn't get there from here anyhow, even if there was someplace to go," Sam continues.

There is more laughter. The crowd is alive and Sam is leading them on. "We've been trying to get here all day from Memphis. We stopped over in Marked Tree and asked a man on a mule how to get here. He scratched his head and said, 'Well, you go through Oil Trough . . .' Then he stopped, scratched someplace else and said, 'You know, I don't think you can get there from here.' "

The crowd whoops in delight as Sam continues to poke fun at their location. "Somebody told me Arkansas was the finest place in the world to be from." He catches them this time and they don't know whether to laugh or applaud. Some do both.

Sam finishes his introduction, and Howard begins to pound the piano as they roll into another rollicking song. The electric fan, plugged into the receptacle at the back of the stage, vainly stirs the hot, dusty air. On the far side of the platform is a group of five or six preschool farm kids, sitting cross-legged in front of their parents who stand at the edge of the stage. One little girl, dressed in a dirty hand-me-down dress that hangs below her knees, is clapping enthusiastically in time with the music. Everyone in Batesville enjoys gospel music.

Howard introduces a song from the new album featuring "Brother Rusty." Then he says to the enthusiastic crowd, "I wonder how many Christian people we have here tonight. Let's see your hands." He catches the audience unawares. A few respond immediately but most are confused. A woman on the third row looks in both directions to see if her neighbors have their hands up and then reluctantly raises hers. One of the deputy sheriffs who has been standing in the front row of the overflow crowd at the side hangs his head and gingerly lifts his hand about halfway—hoping, no doubt, that God will see it but none of his buddies will. A woman on the first row suddenly decides it's time to tie her little boy's shoe string and thus occupies her hands. Vestel surveys the vacillating crowd, her eyes sparkling. She enjoys the fact that Howard has suddenly put them on an uncomfortable spot. If there's one thing the Goodmans believe in, it is taking a stand. None of this riding the fence for them.

Howard shucks his coat and throws it on top of the old piano. It's obvious he's getting ready to preach.

"Now I don't know about all of you. From the looks of things some of you aren't too sure. But I want you to know that I'm a Christian. I ain't ashamed of it either. All of the Goodmans here are Christians. We believe in living what we sing about. We love the Lord and are proud to be able to travel this great country of ours talking and singing about Jesus."

The crowd appreciates his sincerity and is relieved that the center of attention is on Howard's relationship with God—not their own.

"I'm also proud to be an American," Howard says, wiping his big brow with his handkerchief. This time everyone is in agree-

ment. The heavy round of applause indicates they're glad the
emphasis has changed from religion to patriotism.

Howard gestures toward the nearby midway. "Now you take
those young folks over there. They think they're having a good
time. They think that noise, lights, and motion—food, fun, and
sex—is really living. But I want to tell you tonight that real living is only found in Jesus Christ. Tomorrow when those young
people wake up, all they'll have will be a headache from the
booze and a heartache from the guilt. But brother, when we
wake up in the morning (and we'll have to drive all night) our
hearts will be full of joy because we're living for Jesus."

The concert continues with several guitar pieces by Ernie.
Howard and Vestel slip off the stage and wander into the
shadows behind the pavilion. There is a long, sloping hill
crowned with white oaks, hickory, and poplar trees. The eastern sky is dominated by a large, yellow Arkansas moon.

Howard reaches over and takes Vestel's hand. They stand
alone in the darkness, breathing the fresh night air and looking
up at the moon. "Thank you, Jesus," murmurs Vestel as she
squeezes Howard's huge fingers. "Yes, praise you, God," sighs
Howard.

Both stand in silence for a long moment, drinking in the indescribable beauty of the awesome heavens. The moonbeams
tumble softly through the Indian summer sky, filter through the
leaves, and sparkle gently at their feet. A soft breeze whispers
through the tops of the trees, and Vestel moves closer to her
husband and holds his hand tightly with hers.

"Praise Your name, Father, for Your wonderful grace." And
then, in a motion so characteristic of her stage stance, she lifts
the other hand, still clutching her crumpled handkerchief,
toward heaven. Their figures, blending as one, are silhouetted
against the sky. Behind them the noise of the carnival seems to
hush, and only the plaintive strains of Ernie's guitar waft
through the stillness of the night.

> So I'll cherish the old rugged cross
> Till my trophies at last I lay down;

I will cling to the old rugged cross,
And exchange it some day for a crown.

ATLANTA, GEORGIA

Gospel singing is always big in Atlanta. The old city auditorium with its two tiers of balconies seating almost seven thousand is about two-thirds full. People from all walks of life are present. Men with jeweled tiepins and ladies with diamond necklaces sit beside folks wearing cotton pants and flowered dresses.

The Goodmans arrive early Saturday afternoon. They will leave as soon as the concert is over and drive all night to get to Madisonville the next morning in time for church. Because of this they have agreed to surrender their regular feature spot on the program (the last group to sing before intermission) to the Oak Ridge Boys. They will also use the Oak Ridge sound system so they won't have to unload and load before leaving for the long drive through the night.

Warren Roberts, manager of radio WYZE, is the master of ceremonies. He comes on stage dressed in white bucks and flashy sport jacket. After the welcome, he introduces a group known as the VII Romans who finish with a fast rendition of the popular song, "Jesus Is Coming Soon." The audience is alive, and there is good response to this lively instrumental group.

Next are the Kingsmen Quartet followed by the Downings. Both groups do their own rendition of "Jesus Is Coming Soon." The Florida Boys come on strong with an opening number and then swing into Tommy Atwood's popular fiddle arrangement of "Power in the Blood" and a humorous arrangement of "Daddy Sang Bass" in which Derrell Stewert mimics the words with his mouth while the deep bass singer Billy Todd sings behind his hand.

Steve Sanders is next. He's a big favorite with the Atlanta crowd that is made up of many young people. Steve sings a few old numbers including "When the Roll Is Called Up Yonder." Stepping to the front of the stage, he motions for the audience to clap in unison. They oblige and approximately ten thousand hands can be seen clapping vigorously as Steve sings.

Vestel is standing in the wings talking to promoter J. G. Whitfield. She nods at Steve and says, "You know, Whit, Steve rode with us on the bus last week. He sat there for hours between Nashville and Tampa reading his Bible. He told me, 'These other groups may go mod, but I want to keep singing the simple songs.' It really warmed my heart."

Whitfield nods his head knowingly and runs his finger across his pencil thin mustache. "A lot of kids think they have to sing what's being played on the juke boxes," he drawls. "Steve is the perfect example of how a young boy can stick to the old-time music and still be a success. Listen to that crowd. They really love him."

Steve has finished, and the announcer brings on the Happy Goodmans. The ovation even before the Goodmans arrive on-stage is proof of their popularity in Atlanta.

Howard hits the keyboard and the group moves into "O Happy Day." Flashbulbs puncture the darkness as people raise cameras to their eyes. All over the auditorium people begin clapping in spontaneous rhythm.

Howard turns to the mike. "There's gonna be a lot of people in heaven and I'm thankful I'll be there. Listen as Sister Vestel sings, 'This Is Just What Heaven Means to Me.' "

The song is over and Howard shouts, "All who want to go to heaven say 'Amen.' "

There is a thunderous roar from the crowd. "Aaa-men!"

"Now folks, let's listen while Brother Rusty sings something that we've never done onstage before. It's become a favorite on our last album, and we want to do it for you."

All the lights go out except for a lone spotlight that picks up Rusty's head and shoulders onstage. The soft guitar and piano music form the backdrop as Rusty begins to recite softly, "Guilty of Love in the First Degree." The tears glisten from his face as he talks in meter with the music. He finishes and there is total darkness. Then a soft red spotlight picks out the form of a wooden cross on the far side of the stage. There are gasps from the crowd and then audible sobs as the full impact of the cross comes to the hearts of those present.

Almost immediately the tempo changes as the Goodmans swing into "The Sweetest Song I Know." The audience is clapping in rhythm and the beat increases. Finally, exhausted, they stop and leave the stage. The clapping continues and grows louder, and they emerge from the back curtains and take a bow. Warren Roberts calls them back for an unusual third curtain call. The audience just won't stop applauding, and finally Howard sits down at the piano, his coat hanging open like the flaps on a circus tent. The rest of the Goodmans join him at the microphones as they swing into "When Morning Sweeps the Sky."

Sam comes to the mike. "I want to tell you something. Had it not been for the grace of God the Goodmans wouldn't be here tonight. We'd still be back in the sand hills of Alabama living in dirt poverty. God had a purpose for us. He's carried us a long way, but we're the first to recognize that it's all because of His goodness and not because of any talent we might have. We've been blessed tonight, just by being able to tell you about God's goodness, grace, and wonderful love."

NASHVILLE, TENNESSEE

Jubilee, Jubilee, you're invited to this happy jubilee.
Praise the Lord I've been invited to the meeting in the air.
Jubilee! Jubilee!
And the saints of all the ages in their glory will be there.
Jubilee! Jubilee!

Nashville: "The music capital of the world."

The recording studio at WSIX-TV is a mass of sound and movement. This is the same studio that has recorded such greats as Chet Atkins, Eddy Arnold, Al Hirt, Elvis Presley, Jimmy Dean, and the Lamplighters. It was here that Pat Boone began his singing career, and it is here that the "Gospel Singing Jubilee," featuring the Florida Boys, the Dixie Echoes, Steve Sanders,

and the Happy Goodman Family is recorded on TV tape to be
sent out on a weekly basis to scores of stations all over the nation.
The ceiling is crowded with a mazed jumble of huge lights
housed in awkward black cases. Opposite the recording area and
high above the floor is the glassed-in engineer's booth. It's Tuesday morning and almost time to start the day's recording.

In a small room to one side two girls are working quietly and
efficiently with cosmetics. Shadow lines and wrinkles disappear
under the heavy application of creams, powders, pancake make-
up, and mascara.

Vestel and Sam emerge from the small room. Sam has tissue
tucked into his collar around his neck to keep the still-moist
make-up from rubbing off on his shirt collar. Vestel is frowning.
"I hate this stuff. I never have liked cosmetics anyway and
neither does Howard. He likes me like I am. But you've got to
have it under those lights."

Sam grins. "The only thing I don't like is not being able to
scratch my nose when it itches. I've gotta use my pocket knife
and that just don't look very nice in public."

Vestel takes a seat beside Howard on a metal folding chair in
the shadow of a huge stage clown made of fiberboard. Howard,
dressed in a bright, strawberry-colored shirt with matching flowered tie and green striped pants, is talking to one of the guitar
players from the Dixie Echoes.

"Man, the fish were really bitin' last week. Ernie's kid caught
a four-pounder, and Ernie's been trying to get him to swap fishing rigs ever since."

Derrell Stewert, the pianist for the Florida Boys, walks to the
center of the room holding up Howard's coat. "Man, look what
I found hanging over the back of the chair. You all oughta see
this. There must be ten yards of cloth in this tent." He holds up
the dark green, pin-stripe suitcoat.

Howard leans back and laughs. "It takes a man to fill a coat
like that, Sonny. Maybe one day you'll grow up."

"If I grow up that big, I think I'd rather stay a little boy."

"Well, at the rate you're going you'll probably get your wish."

Derrell laughs and starts to put on Howard's coat that drapes over him like a poncho.

"Besides," says Howard, "at least I haven't grown clear through my hair and have to wear a toupee like some fellows I know."

A baby grand piano has been wheeled into the studio and pushed into position. Behind a small draw curtain Ricky mounts his drums and begins a slow rhythm beat. Ricky likes to record for TV because he doesn't have to go through make-up. He'll sit behind the curtain and play for all the singing groups. In fact, most of the instrumentalists will "trade off" and play behind the scenes for the various singing groups.

Les Beasley, who acts as host and director of "Jubilee," is sitting at a small table going over the format. Six one-hour programs are scheduled for recording—to be taped in fifteen-minute segments.

The colored panels are pushed in place. Camera time is near. The monstrous light-control panel with its banks of switches winks on and off as the technician adjusts the overhead lights from the rear of the studio. He lowers the rheostat and the house lights go dim. The mikes are in place and the "stay tuned" signs are in position.

Howard, still sitting on the metal chair, looks around at the group and says, "Praise God, boys, I'm ready to go."

There are last minute touches with the hairbrushes and some of the men sneak back in the corner for a final shot of hair spray. Neck tissues are discarded. A muffled voice comes from the control booth. "Give me an audio level."

Les Beasley calls for the Florida Boys to take positions behind the microphones. They break into song. "Okay, we're ready, Les," says the voice from the control booth.

"Hey, that's not fair," growls Billy Todd. "I just got on pitch and they cut me off."

The anonymous muffled voice from the overhead speaker comes on again. "All set, Les, let's roll." There is a distinct click from the speaker and then another voice begins the countdown. "Nine, eight, seven, six, five, four, three . . ." The voice fades as the camera crew chief, standing with two other men behind their cameras in the center of the room, raises his finger and points at Les. The red eye blinks on, and Les's smooth voice comes through the overhead speakers.

"Welcome to the 'Gospel Singing Jubilee' featuring the world's greatest gospel singers. To begin our program we'll hear from the Florida Boys singing a song written by Rusty Goodman, 'Had It Not Been.' "

"Good. Cut," says the voice from the booth. The Florida Boys take their places behind the mikes as Les moves into his slot with them. A pause and then, "Okay, counting." The loud click is heard again and the recorded voice begins the countdown again. "Nine, eight, seven, six, five, four, three . . ." The finger is up and pointing. The red light blinks on, and the camera focuses in on Derrell Stewert's flashing white teeth. His fingers fly up and down the keyboard. The camera chief points at the left camera, and the red light flashes on picking up the quartet as they blend their voices in Rusty's searchingly beautiful spiritual ballad.

To one side, Ernie and the two guitarists from the Dixie Echoes lend instrumental support. Behind the curtain Ricky's soft drums give the needed beat. It's a team effort although the Florida Boys are the only ones on camera.

The voice from the control booth asks for Steve Sanders. "Give us a voice level." The cameras swing one hundred eighty degrees and focus in on Steve who sits nonchalantly on a stool in the middle of the studio holding a mike. Much of the singing done in the recording studio is pantomime, and he is a master of this. The orchestra comes in over the speakers, and Steve's recorded voice blends with the silent moving of his lips. Only an expert could tell whether he is actually singing or not. During the difficult parts when synchronization is liable to be slightly "off," the camera may switch to one of the several landscape pictures that stand on an easel. Occasionally these pictures will be super-imposed over a close-up of Steve "singing" to help with the visual effect and lessen the danger that some sharp television viewer will recognize that he's pantomiming.

The voice level is complete. "Okay. Good. Roll 'em."

"Nine, eight, seven, six, five, four, three . . ."

Two cameras are on Steve; one will give a close-up and the other will superimpose a distance shot. The third camera is pointing at Ernie's hands on the guitar. Les's voice comes over the speaker, "Now we'll hear from Steve Sanders . . ." The monitor set shows Ernie's fingers as he pantomimes the guitar music. Suddenly the red lights on the other two cameras blink on, and Steve raises his head and moves his lips in synchronization to the music.

It's time for the Goodmans. Howard seats himself at the piano, his ham-hock sized hands resting gently on the keyboard. Vestel takes her place between Sam and Rusty, and Bobby and Ernie stand back to one side, guitars slung at "ready." From the control booth comes the anonymous voice, "Okay, ready for the Goodmans." Les makes his introduction, and the camera backs off and focuses on Howard whose smiling face and bouncing hands signal the beginning of a musical treat that will set the entire nation to tapping their feet. It's Howard's own composition, "Give Up."

The song closes but Vestel isn't through. Throwing one hand in the air, she starts the chorus all over. The guitarists are with her and the group joins in as they pick up the beat. By the time they finish, everyone is glad to see the camera focus in on the stationary sign that says, "More to Come."

"Time to shoot a closing," says the voice in the control booth. The three singing groups take their places on the multilevel risers. "Places everyone."

Les's prerecorded voice comes over the microphone, "This has been the 'Gospel Singing Jubilee' featuring . . ." The signature music comes through the loudspeakers and each singer moves his lips in pantomime:

Jubilee! Jubilee,
You're invited to this happy jubilee.

WHEATON, MARYLAND

The Silver Eagle weaves its way through the heavy Saturday afternoon traffic of suburban Washington, D.C., and pulls up in front of Northwood High School. A large sign outside says, "Gospel Singing Concert." Sam is driving, and he grunts emphatically as he heaves at the wheel, pulling the bus into the narrow alley behind the building.

Ricky bounces out and goes to check the gymnasium. He comes back giving directions on where to enter. However, his judgment is off since the large speakers can't be fitted through the double doors because of a middle brace. Rusty quickly produces a screwdriver, and while the school janitor stands by twisting his hands in concern, Rusty proceeds to unscrew the restraining screws and remove the center support in the doorway.

The spacious gym, with the stage on one end, is ready. Eighteen hundred metal folding chairs have been placed on the playing floor. To the far side the collapsible bleachers have been lowered, providing space for another two hundred and fifty. The plexiglass basketball backboards have been raised at each end and the curtains opened. A lone Wurlitzer spinet piano sits on stage.

Rusty moves to the piano while Ernie tunes his guitar. The gymnasium is rapidly filling with well-dressed spectators.

Rusty shakes his head as Sam enters. "Bad situation tonight. No piano."

Sam stalks around the piano chewing at a toothpick. "Spinet," he grumbles.

"Not only that, but it's out of tune," Rusty adds.

"Isn't there another one in the school?" Sam asks. "Why do we get stuck with the sorriest piano?"

"Yep. There's a Baldwin grand back there locked up in a room, but we can't use it. Some official said it was to be used for 'high-class' functions only. Last week they used it for a concert that thirty-five people attended."

Sam shakes his head and walks back to the bus to get dressed.

Already more than a thousand people have crowded into the gym and there is still thirty minutes to go before curtain time.

The noise from the huge gymnasium is subdued, but warm and friendly. Howard is busy at the record table talking to the crowd of fans and selling records—lots of them—which is unusual before the concert. But something indicates that this is not going to be a "usual" concert.

The young promoter is on the stage, and after leading the audience in a song, he says, "This is our first gospel singing concert and we've invited the very best in the nation to be with us, the Happy Goodmans." The crowd begins to applaud loudly. "First though, we have some other groups that will thrill your heart and set your feet to tapping."

The first group sings four quick songs and then unexpectedly leaves the stage. The promoter is in the back of the gym checking ticket sales. The stage is empty. Sam, standing behind the record rack to one side, shouts loudly. "You want me to say a few words?" The audience roars in approval and laughter. The promoter runs the length of the gym to the stage. "I didn't know they were going to quit," he pants to the audience. "They must have run out of songs."

The audience forgives with more laughter.

The Wootens, a Pentecostal group from Kentucky, are next. Even though not as formally organized as most singing groups, they are a favorite of the Goodmans. "They're genuine Christians," Vestel nods.

The three Wooten sisters, dressed in bright mango orange dresses, hair long, without make-up, come to the stage. They are joined by their cousin Hamp who rounds out the quartet. One of the girls takes her place at the piano and they move into their first song.

Rusty, who is probably gospel music's finest soloist, considers Hamp Wooten to be the best "fire-eatin' singer" in the field. Hamp, his left leg crippled in a childhood accident, stands between the two girls. Their music arrangement is strictly ad lib, but filled with life and vitality. The audience recognizes it immediately and catches the spirit during the first song.

The Wootens finish singing after four selections and leave the stage. However, the audience is not finished and calls them back. Hamp steps to the microphone. It's the first time any of them have spoken. "We were raised down in the hills of Kentucky, in case you didn't know." His hillbilly twang shows he's authentic and the people applaud. "But I'm so glad that God's people is the best friends I've got."

Hamp begins to sing and the girls step forward and join him.

My burdens keep me humble
And they teach me to pray . . .

There is a special feeling about the entire room. These people are sincere. There's none of the usual "showmanship" about them. They finish singing, bow their heads, and quickly leave the stage.

Again the audience calls them back. Vestel, now backstage in the wings, says to the young promoter, "See what I mean. Those kids are real. The audience knows it too. You can't fool folks out there. I tried to tell J. D. Sumner that last year. He just laughed and said the audience doesn't see anything but what's before them on stage. I said, 'J. D., you can't come backstage and use the Lord's name in vain and then go out there and expect God to bless you.' "

The Wootens sing their final song and the master of ceremonies is back on the stage. "Tonight you're going to hear the greatest gospel singers in the world."

The Goodmans hit the stage like a hurricane. Howard's hands begin playing even before he's fully settled on the piano bench.

Oooooo, Happy Day!
O Happy Day!
When Jesus washed my sins away!
He taught me how to watch and pray
And live rejôicing every day;
O Happy Day!

O Happy Day!
When Jesus washed my sins away!

The music comes to a fast close, and Howard turns to the enthusiastic audience. "Some of you all ain't clapped yet." This brings down the house in applause.

"How many of you are from out of town?"

Nearly all hands are raised.

Sam jokes, "We'd of been better off holding this meeting out of town."

Howard says, "How many from Wheaton?" There is a long pause; then he says, "Yes, sister, I see your hand out there." The audience applauds good-naturedly.

Howard continues. "I'm so happy the Wootens are here tonight. They're such dear friends. I tried to call them earlier in the week and the phone rang and rang and finally Naomi answered. She was all out of breath."

Sam interrupts. "It's hard to climb that telephone pole out there in the woods."

Howard continues. "No, but all three girls were up on the roof repairing shingles on the barn."

He turns back to the piano, and they move into a bouncing rendition of another song. The crowd is clapping in time.

They finish the first verse and chorus and Rusty takes the mike. "How many Christians do we have here tonight?" Most hands are immediately raised. Someone far back in the crowd shouts, "Hallelujah!"

"How many of you have been to a camp meeting?"

Almost as many hands are raised again.

"Then let's give a wave offering to the Lord tonight. Reach down in that pocketbook and get a handkerchief. If you can't find a handkerchief, get a piece of paper. On this next chorus, wave a sign to the Lord. They demonstrate on the streets of Washington and Baltimore by waving signs. Let's demonstrate by waving a handkerchief for the Lord."

The music swings back into high gear, and a thousand hands are seen waving handkerchiefs, sweaters, papers. One woman is standing, waving her purse. It is an impressive sight, and even after the music is over some remain standing, heads back in ecstasy, still waving slowly.

Howard says with great emotion, "Praise the Lord." Then he looks out at the audience and says, "Say it with me, Praise the Lord." The great crowd responds with an even greater roar.

Howard is grinning as he speaks into the mike. "A woman called Sister Vestel awhile back and said, 'My doctor told me not to get emotional. If I come to your church will I get excited?' Vestel answered, 'Honey, you'd have a nervous breakdown in the first few minutes.' "

Sam goes into his introductions, and then the crowd is lifted to their feet as the Goodmans break out into Sam's composition of "Big Homecoming." As the music gets faster and faster, Sam jumps off the front of the stage and walks up and down the aisle, the microphone cord trailing after him. The audience is clapping loudly in time to the music and even though it is time for intermission, they are reluctant to stop for the break.

After intermission the Wootens are back onstage. Sam comes out and interrupts before they can sing. "First time I met the Wootens I was singing at a camp meeting in Kentucky. I had finished and was sitting way back in the tabernacle when the leader asked if anyone else wanted to sing. The Wooten sisters came out and heaven swung low. I thought, 'I came here to work, but I'm being blessed beyond all measure.' "

Sam leaves the stage and the Wootens begin. Ricky and Bobby appear behind them, Ricky on the drums and Bobby with his bass guitar. Sam walks back on carrying the rhythm guitar, and the instrumental accompaniment is added to the vocalist's rendition of "A Man Asked Me How to Make It to Heaven."

Naomi Wooten takes the mike. "Goodmans brag on everyone, but no one brags on them. Probably because they're jealous. But I want to say thank God for the Happy Goodmans. That first year at camp meetin' us three girls was singing. We didn't have no money. We didn't have no job and daddy was laid off work. We didn't even have money to get home. Howard got up at the close of the meetin' and said, 'God is laying it on my heart to give the Wootens some money.' Oh, I thank God for 'em. Our next album will be recorded in the Goodmans' studio in Madisonville. I know it'll be great because anything the Goodmans does is great."

Naomi isn't through. She begins to talk about Jesus and His second coming. Her voice builds to a fever pitch as she preaches. The crowd begins to shout with her. "Amen!" "Hallelujah!" "Praise God!" Then suddenly Naomi breaks into song. "I stood on the banks of Jordan . . ."

The program is over, but the cross has been made real tonight—not only in song but in the lives of those singing. It is always that way, however, when you follow the Eagle.

MADISONVILLE, KENTUCKY

There's gonna be a big homecoming
I'll meet you up in heaven
At that big homecoming in the sky;
There's gonna be a great big table spread,
Milk and honey fed
At that big homecoming in the sky.

—words and music by
Sam Goodman

It's the Sunday before Labor Day at New Life Temple. To say the least, things are "hopping." It's annual homecoming for the Goodman family.

The church parking lot and the parking lot of the National Guard Armory next door are jammed with cars from all over the nation. Every motel room in town is taken. Despite the somewhat negative attitude some of the townspeople hold toward the Goodmans, homecoming at New Life Temple is still the biggest event of the year in Madisonville.

The building at New Life Temple is a fabulous piece of architecture. Sitting on a beautiful hill overlooking the city park and reservoir, the church has an aura of grace and beauty.

Inside, it is shaped like a big piece of pie with the choir loft and baptistry in the apex. The tremendous velvet-covered pulpit is custom constructed in a wraparound style to fit Howard's shape. To the left of the pulpit is a beautiful Hammond organ and on the opposite side sits a grand piano. Microphones are everywhere, hanging from the ceiling and on stands across the platform. The Goodmans like sound—loud and on key. The pews are covered with red velvet to match the brilliant red carpet on the floor. Everything in the building gives the impression of life—new life.

The meeting has already started, and the auditorium is packed with people. Chairs down the side aisles and down the center aisles help seat the crowd, but many people are still standing.

Joel Hemphill, Howard's nephew by marriage, is on the platform. "I've been in church all my life, but you know what, it never ceases to thrill my soul when I'm going to the house of the Lord."

There are loud shouts of "Amen!" as he continues. "It's plumb exciting. I feel like I'm on the winning side.

"Now we want to sing one of our songs that the Goodmans have recorded. It's called 'Pity the Man.' "

Joel finishes amid shouts of "Praise the Lord" and "Amen." He introduces his group, which includes his beautiful wife, LaBreeska.

Next Vestel, dressed in a flame-red dress which matches the carpet, introduces her sisters from Alabama. "Now I want to introduce my brother Cat. He's not one of the greatest, he is *the* greatest tenor in gospel singing.

"When I was a kid learning how to sing, Cat taught me not to sing sharp or flat by paddling me if I did. He's retired now and lives on a farm down in Alabama, but if you don't hear anything else today, it will have been worth your time to come hear Cat sing."

Vestel is right about Cat Freeman. He does have a great tenor voice. As he moves into the second chorus, the choir, seated behind him, breaks out into spontaneous song. The men on the platform pick up their instruments and the entire room is filled with music.

As he finishes, Howard steps forward again. "The Happy Goodmans are going to sing a song. It's the sweetest song I know." Suddenly this Sunday morning congregation of almost two thousand people is transformed into a clapping, shouting, swaying group of excited worshipers.

As the song closes, Howard comes to one of the platform microphones and says with a long wheeze, "My, you folks are making me hoarse, but I praise God for it." Catching his breath he continues, "I want to introduce the sweetest mother in all the world. She's sitting right down here where she always sits in church. Mama Goodman." The congregation applauds as Mama Goodman, still spry and straight although with snowy white hair, stands to her feet.

It's time for the sermon. Howard introduces his uncle, Herschel Nix, whom he has invited to preach the homecoming sermon. "Uncle Herschel is a shouter," Howard laughs. "He speaks in two tones—loud and louder. I know you'll love him."

If there is any doubt as to whether Howard was exaggerating or not, it is all dispelled when Uncle Herschel stands to preach. In thunderous tones he reads his text: "For as the lightning cometh out of the east, and shineth even unto the west; so shall also the coming of the Son of Man be."

"When I preaches I gets filled up," he shouts. "And this morning I'm running over as I want to talk about that great homecoming in the sky when Jesus returns again."

Uncle Herschel's voice rises in a magnificent crescendo of volume and intensity. Like a giant tidal wave rushing before an erupting volcano, he soars to oratorical heights, crashing down on accented words and blasting off to new elevations of verbal splendor. The people respond by shouting, clapping, and raising their hands.

Uncle Herschel is now going full blast, his words coming forth like machine-gun volleys punctuated by deafening blasts from heavy artillery. The people are backing him up shouting,

"Preach it, brother!" There's no doubt about the fact that this man means business for his Lord.

The sermon isn't long, although it makes up for its brevity in intensity. He finishes and the congregation stands to its feet to sing a final song. Howard announces the picnic which is to take place across the street in the park. "And don't forget to come back after you eat. The best is yet to come."

Directly across the street from the church building is a grassy park with concrete block shelters. A big table is covered with piles of barbecued pork, pots of baked beans, and potato salad. The hot Labor Day sun streams through the leaves of the trees on the happy crowd below, as more than two thousand people file through the line heaping their plates with the delicious food.

After eating, the people return to the building. Other singers have arrived and the room is even more crowded than it was for the morning service. Sam is the master of ceremonies as the program gets under way.

"Let me hear everyone shout 'Amen' real good," he says. There is a loud cry of "Amen." "Now let's stand and sing about the amazing grace of God. While we sing, let's lift our hands to the Lord and really praise Him."

Next Howard calls all the ordained ministers in the crowd to the platform. Seven men take seats on the platform and various singers come to the stage to perform.

Then a roll call of the states. Pennsylvania, Wisconsin, Illinois, Ohio, Missouri, Alabama, Florida, South Carolina, Texas—all in all there are nineteen states represented. "There's a woman here from Denver, Colorado, just to attend this service," a female voice in the congregation shouts. A woman stands up and raises her hand. There is a roar of applause.

"There's not a motel or hotel that has a vacant room today. Every place is filled."

The Life Temple choir sings and the congregation joins in. The choir is weaving back and forth, clapping and bouncing. Drums, guitar, piano, organ, even a tambourine are going full blast. Mama Goodman is on her feet, shouting and clapping.

The music dies and Vestel grabs a microphone and begins to preach.

It's 5:00 P.M. and the group is exhausted. They drove all the night before from Atlanta and no one had any sleep. They close out with a climaxing note by singing Sam's rendition of "Big Homecoming," and Howard finally dismisses the crowd.

"We've had a great time today," Howard sighs as the people begin to leave. "But thank God homecoming don't come but once a year. I just don't think I could stand it more often."

New Life Temple, Madisonville, Kentucky

Bobby, Howard, Vestel, Sam, Rusty, and the Silver Eagle

Sam, Vestel, Rusty, Howard

Vestel

Howard

Recording "live" in Nashville

Sam, Rusty, Eddie Crook, Howard at Waco Concert, January 1972

Sam, Vestel, Rusty, Howard

Sam, Vestel, Rusty, Ernie Maxwell, Bob Goodman
at piano—Howard

Larry Strzelecki, Sam, Vestel, Rusty, Eddie Crook, Howard

Daddy

Mama

Sam, Ruth, Rusty, Gussie Mae, Stella Mae, Eloise, Howard

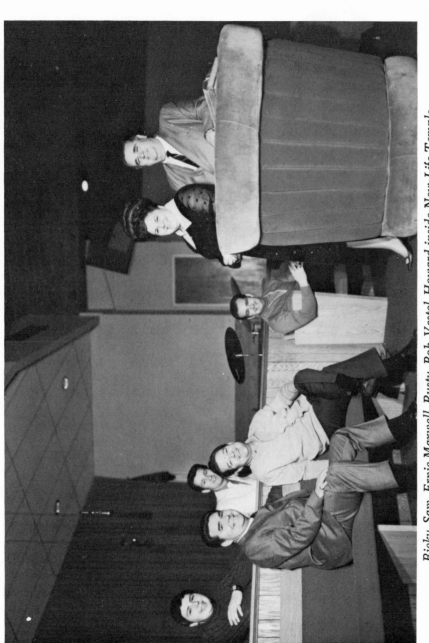

Ricky, Sam, Ernie Maxwell, Rusty, Bob, Vestel, Howard inside New Life Temple

Part Two
How It All Began

INTRODUCTION

I wish everybody could meet Howard Goodman in person. A tall man with huge head, jowls, neck, and shoulders, his arms are the size of sawed-off telephone poles, and he sprouts a crop of curly hair that is turning gray and always needing to be trimmed around the ears.

When he walks, though, it is with a bounce that emulates not only great power, but deep joy. Even when he's angry, he smiles. And Howard gets angry—at sin. Yet, even when he's standing in the New Life Temple in Madisonville, roaring his displeasure at Satan and smashing his tremendous fist against the reinforced top of the custom-designed, barrel-shaped pulpit, there's still a twinkle in his eye.

Howard is best known, of course, crouched over the keyboard of a studio piano that seems to struggle in vain to compete with him for size, throwing his great head back and thumping his huge ham-hock hands up and down on the keys while his voice roars or whispers the message of gospel music. And when he gives a long, asthmatic-style wheeze and turns to the audience, his great tent-sized coat flapping loosely in front of him, and says with a grin, "Praise the Lord, folks," there's no mistaking why he is known all over the nation as "Happy" Goodman.

But things haven't always been this way. The Goodman story (and to get it straight, we'll have to let Howard tell it in his own words) goes back many years to the poverty-stricken coal-mining hills of north Alabama. There, at the close of World War I, Sam and Gussie Goodman started raising a family. Their first son was called Willie Howard. That's where the story begins. Where it

71

ends, only God knows. But wherever, all of us are banking that it will be with the words of Rusty's famous song, "I wouldn't take nothing for my journey now."

JAMIE BUCKINGHAM

Chapter One

I've dreamed many a dream that's never come true,
I've seen many of them vanish at dawn;
But I've realized enough of my dreams, thank God!
To make me want to keep dreaming on.

I don't regret a mile I travel for the Lord;
I don't regret the times I trusted in His Word;
I've seen the years go by, many days without a song;
But I don't regret a mile I travel for the Lord.

HOWARD GOODMAN

It's seven miles from Dora to Cordova—that is, if you follow the railroad track. The only other way is to take the dirt road that runs south through Flat Creek, cross the Big Warrior River on the ferry, and then go back up the mountain and come into Cordova from the Birmingham side.

When Uncle Herschel and Aunt Flossie sent word across the mountain from Burnwell Switch that Great-grandpa Sargeant had died, mama began to make immediate plans to get into town to attend the wake.

"I don't mind sitting up all night at one of those 'wakes,'" daddy muttered as he got dressed, "but it's a dadgum shame it ain't grandpa instead of great-grandpa. I'd heap rather attend his funeral."

Now mama didn't usually cross daddy. But this was one sore spot that always made her mad. She whirled around and put her hands on her hips. She was twenty-five years younger than

73

daddy and knew the animosity that existed between him and her father. But she wasn't going to put up with daddy's surliness.

"I'll thank you, Sam Goodman, not to talk that way about my daddy."

"Aw, Gussie, I really didn't mean it. It's just that grandpa is so mean . . ."

"That's enough. I mean it. God's gonna punish you for talking that way one of these days."

Daddy had moved to Samoset from Birmingham eleven years ago and had given up his job as head porter at the Tutwiler Hotel to go to work as a guard for the mine workers' union. He was a Spanish-American War veteran who had married a Spanish girl in the Philippines and stayed on in the islands after the war was over. But when his first wife died, he moved back to the states with his son. After the boy was grown, daddy settled down with his job at the Tutwiler and his Spanish-American War pension. However, when the union asked him to move up to Samoset, forty miles north of Birmingham, to act as a guard at the DeBardeleban coal mine during the big strike in 1920, he accepted.

That was where he met mama. Grandpa Sargeant, mama's daddy, owned a couple of big sawmills down in the hollow just below Jasper. Mama used to ford two creeks and walk up to the post office at the mining camp where daddy was on guard. She was twenty-five years old at the time and daddy was fifty, but it didn't take long for them to fall in love and run away and get married.

Grandpa Sargeant never forgave daddy for stealing his daughter. "That old man," he used to mutter, "can you imagine the likes of him coming up here from Birmingham and stealing my baby?"

"Grandpa, your baby was twenty-five years old and I didn't steal her. She gave herself to me."

That was usually as far as he ever got with the conversation, for grandpa would head back in the house to get his shotgun and daddy would take off down the road.

Now it was eleven years and five children later, but the feeling still ran strong.

"We're going to Cordova to sit up with your great-grandfather's corpse," mama said to us kids. "And your daddy better watch what he says to grandpa or he'll be hearing from me for a long time to come." The last part of the sentence, although spoken to us, was directed toward daddy—and we knew it.

We were poor. In fact, poverty was a way of life for us. A pair of bib overalls was like owning a tuxedo. The girls wore dresses made from flour sacks, and I had some old hand-me-downs from some of the cousins. None of the children had any shoes. Mama had washed out our few rags and scrubbed each child down that afternoon. "We may be poor, but that's no excuse to be filthy," mama would say as she'd scrub our ears and the backs of our necks. The cold spring water, poured from a wooden bucket over our half-naked bodies, was enough to bring the dead back to life. But mama was determined that none of her children were going to show up at a wake in dirty clothes or with dirty ears.

"Let's get started," daddy hollered from the yard. He was standing beside the door with the baby buggy. It was an old, blue buggy that he had swapped from Tom Anderson over in Sipsey for the crosstree on a two-horse wagon. It had been in the family as long as I could remember, one of the few items of furniture that continued to follow us around as we moved every few months from one place to another.

Mama picked up Ruth, the baby, and carried her outside and plopped her in the buggy. She was followed by Eloise, who was just a toddler, Stella, then Gussie Mae, and finally me—Willie Howard. At ten years of age I was the oldest and thus qualified to bring up the rear.

Daddy stood stiffly in the yard dressed in his starched white shirt with high celluloid collar, a carry-over from his days at the Tutwiler. His flat-top straw hat was perched on top of a white thatch of hair.

"We best be getting on toward town. It'll be dark before long, and I want to get across the trestle while we can still see."

The trestle was the awesome railroad bridge that spanned the Big Warrior River just outside Cordova. Almost half a mile long, it connected the tops of two mountains one hundred feet above the sluggish black water.

We cut through the woods and climbed the embankment to the railroad tracks, heading west toward Cordova and reaching the trestle just at dusk. It was a single-track trestle with open crossties spaced about two feet apart. Daddy parked the baby buggy beside the tracks. Turning to me he said, "Willie Howard, you carry the baby and I'll carry Eloise."

Daddy started out on the trestle, walking gingerly between the two steel tracks, placing his feet firmly on each crosstie. Mama, right behind him, hesitated. "Sam, I don't like the looks of this," she said, peering into the gathering dusk at the far side of the bridge. Far below the misty river swirled around a great bend in the valley. A light fog was rising from the murky surface. "If one of these children slipped, they'd fall through the crossties and be gone forever."

"Now, mama, it's gonna be all right. You just hold on to my arm and we'll be across in a few minutes. Then I'll come back and get the buggy and we'll go on up to grandpa's."

"I still don't like it," mama said, but she held tightly to his arm as he picked up Eloise and we moved out onto the trestle. Since I was the biggest child, I brought up the rear with Stella and Gussie Mae holding on in front and Ruth in my arms.

"What if we get out here in the middle and a train comes along," mama stuttered. "Sam, I think we ought to go back."

"We're too far out now. You kids be careful and don't stub your toe or pick up a splinter on these crossties."

We continued on, gingerly feeling each step. Far below us in the gathering gloom we could see the swirling water. Mama began to whimper, "Sam, let's go back. I'd just as well wait till morning if it's the same with you."

Daddy chuckled. "I thought you were the one set on going."

"Well, I was. But I forgot what it's like to cross this bridge in the dark."

Suddenly Eloise began to twist and fidget. A swarm of gnats appeared out of nowhere, flying into our eyes, noses, and ears. The children began to slap at their faces and cry.

"Sam, I'm going back," mama cried. "God's going to punish you for what you said about grandpa, and I don't want to be here when it happens."

Daddy started to reply, but just then Eloise reached up and knocked his hat off. He tried to jerk his hand free from mama's grasp to catch it, but it was too late. It fell backward through the crossties and tumbled over and over to the dark water a hundred feet below.

"If you don't hush your crying and keep moving, that's what's gonna happen to you, too." I could hear mama stifling her sniffles as we moved ahead and finally reached the far side.

"Now you all just wait here beside the tracks and I'll be back in a minute with the buggy."

"Sam! Wait!" Mama called out. But daddy had already disappeared into the dusk, his long legs stretching out and taking the crossties two at a time.

The darkness grew thicker over the Alabama mountains, and the only sounds were the night noises of the crickets, frogs, and whippoorwills. The fog was rising slowly from the river, and the first twinkle of the evening star appeared in the darkening sky. Mama busied herself with the girls, straightening their clothes, brushing the dirt and cinders from their faces and hands, and comforting them with soft words. I stood on the rails, my bare feet sliding back and forth along the smooth steel. Far across the valley I could see the dark outline of the mountains.

My eyes finally spotted movement far out on the trestle. I could make out the dim figure of daddy, coming toward us like a spook in the night. He was about halfway across the trestle, still a quarter of a mile away, with the baby buggy over his head covering the upper part of his body. As he came closer, we could see that he was peering downward, looking for each cross-tie and trying to keep his balance in the darkness.

At that same moment I heard another sound. It was the lonesome whistle of a train in the night. The hair stood up on the back of my neck, and I looked down the embankment at mama. She had heard it too, and her eyes were as big as saucers. She began to scramble up the ten-foot embankment that was covered with rock, cinders, and pieces of coal. She finally reached the rails and stood with me, looking out on the trestle at the dim figure of daddy picking his way slowly toward us, looking strangely top heavy with the big baby buggy over his head, the wheels sticking up like horns.

We heard the sound again, only this time it was closer. Mama sucked in her breath, and I felt my stomach begin to knot. "Sam!" mama screamed, "Hurry! Hurry!"

But daddy couldn't hear. The baby buggy was covering his ears, and his vision was limited to the few crossties immediately in front of him.

My bare feet gripped the cold steel of the rails, and I felt a tingling vibration. I had walked the rails enough to know what that meant. The train was getting close. And then we saw it as it thundered around the bend on the far side of the trestle, its light probing the semidarkness, casting weird shadows on the fog rising from the river below. Just then I saw daddy straighten up and slowly turn around, baby buggy and all. At the same time the train cut loose with a mournful blast of the whistle that sounded like the notes of a funeral dirge.

Mama and I screamed louder, and the girls, at the bottom of the embankment, began to cry in fright—although they didn't know what was going on. Daddy didn't need our encouragement to hurry up. Whirling in his tracks he dashed toward us. I could see his leaping figure, with the baby buggy still over his head, silhouetted in the bright light of the onrushing locomotive.

He was still a hundred yards out on the trestle when I felt the tracks begin to vibrate violently and knew the locomotive had started across the bridge on the other side. Mama screamed, "Drop the buggy! Drop the buggy! Drop the buggy!"

But daddy wasn't about to drop the buggy. It was a part of the family just as much as one of the children.

By now the engineer had spotted daddy's running figure and he blew the whistle in a series of short, shrill blasts. The noise— the train whistle, the shouting, the screaming, the roar of the locomotive and the vibration of the trestle—sounded like all the demons of hell had broken loose and were flying up the valley. Daddy's flying figure seemed to be picking up speed as he lengthened his stride to take in four crossties at a time. It was going to be close, and I shut my eyes just as mama pulled me down the embankment.

Looking up I saw daddy clear the end of the trestle with the train only a few feet behind him. Taking a flying leap, he left the tracks and landed stomach first on the rocks and cinders of the steep embankment, rolling over and over to the bottom. The locomotive, whistle still screaming wildly, thundered past, pulling the long line of coal cars behind.

Mama was hysterical with fright. Grabbing daddy, she hugged him, screaming and crying at the same time. "God must have some purpose for saving us," she wept uncontrollably.

Daddy was trying to regain his breath. His shirt was almost torn off, and his face and arms were bloodied from the encounter with the rocks on the railroad bed. Wiping some of the soot and blood from his face, he struggled to his feet while mama clung to his legs and ankles. "Not bad for an old man," he panted. "Too bad grandpa couldn't have seen me then. He might have changed his dadgum mind about me."

Mama's eyes shot sparks of fire. "He'd have changed his mind, all right," she half screamed. "He'd have thought you were all fool rather than just half crazy like he now thinks."

Daddy looked at me and grinned. "Well, let's head on into town. We still have a wake to attend."

Bending over he picked up the baby buggy. It was smashed beyond recognition. He stood there holding the wreckage in his hands and shook his head. "I guess I landed on top of it when I jumped off the tracks," he said.

Mama got smartly to her feet. "That does it," she said. Gath-

ering Ruth in her arms she began to climb the railroad embankment back to the tracks. We fell in line behind. Daddy, still
limping, humbly took his place in the rear as we marched into
town between the rails. The Goodmans had arrived.

The next day, following the wake, Mama didn't feel like walking the seven miles back home. The kids had finally fallen asleep
on pallets on the floor, but the adults had made a full night of
it, talking and visiting over great-grandpa's coffin which occu-
pied front stage center in the living room, supported by a couple
of chairs.

Some of the men took turns sneaking out back and taking a
nip from a jug. Whiskey, of course, was illegal, but moonshine
was plentiful in north Alabama, and almost every home had its
own stock of home-brew stored in quart Mason jars under the
house, in root cellars, or in the attic.

Uncle James, mama's younger brother, was known to imbibe
a little now and then. Especially at wakes. In fact, Uncle James
would invite himself to a wake just to be where the action was.
This night was no exception and by dawn Uncle James was almost as well embalmed as great-grandpa.

Despite his drinking, Uncle James had always been a favorite
of the family. We always figured him as something of a million-
aire because he had saved enough money to buy his own car, a
1926 Ford Model T.

Several years before, he had collided head-on with a switch
engine at a railroad crossing and had come out second best. The
switch engine not only demolished his car but almost demolished
Uncle James. Ever since then he had walked with a horrible
limp on badly twisted legs. Mama used to think that Uncle
James drank because of disfigurement. Daddy liked to remind
her, however, that it was drinking that had actually led to the
disfigurement. Years later, when Uncle James had a conversion
experience and sobered up to become a dedicated Christian, he
confessed that the only accident that led him to drink was the
accident of birth.

The morning after the wake, however, Uncle James volun-

teered to take us home in his two-door Model T. The fact that
he was so drunk he could hardly walk, much less see, didn't
seem to make much difference to mama. Anything was better
than walking back across that trestle—even without the buggy.

All nine of us piled into the little Ford. Uncle James was at
the wheel and Aunt Pet was beside him. Mama sat beside her
with Ruth in her arms and Eloise in her lap. Daddy, me, and the
other girls squeezed in the back seat. We were all wedged in
pretty tight in a car that was only made to hold four people.

Leaving Cordova we crossed the mountain, weaving from one
side of the road to another and thankful that very few of the
people in those parts had been able to save enough money to
buy a car. Finally, cresting the top of the mountain, we started
down the abrupt incline on the other side toward the ferry
docked on the Big Warrior. I could peek out from my cramped
back-seat position and see the swirling waters of the river far
below. The steep road went straight down the mountain and
onto the raft which could be propelled across the river by a
cable from the other side.

As we started down, the car somehow got away from Uncle
James. It may have been that he had one of his blackout spells,
but whatever the cause, the car was out of control and speeding
wildly down the dirt road toward the river below. Uncle James
couldn't get his feet on the brakes. Aunt Pet and mama began
to scream and daddy was standing up in the back seat trying to
reach over Uncle James's shoulders. Meanwhile, Uncle James
was slapping at daddy's hands, sure that everyone was trying to
do him some kind of physical harm. Mama was screaming "Do
something! Do something!" but there wasn't much that could
be done. Everyone was in a state of near hysterics, screaming and
hollering as the car gained speed, rocking back and forth down
the rutted road toward the river below.

The speed and commotion must have slightly sobered Uncle
James. He tried desperately to get his foot on the brake pedal,
but of the three pedals on the floor of the Model T, he never
did seem to be able to find the right one. Once he hit the ac-
celerator and we hurtled forward even faster.

Aunt Pet finally got her foot on top of Uncle James's foot, and just as we flashed through the gate at the ferry, breaking the crossarm like it was a match stick, roaring across the gangplank and out onto the deck of the ferry, the two of them pressed the brakes at the same time and the old car skidded to a halt. The front end was left dangling precariously over the outside edge of the ferry. There we balanced, rocking back and forth over the muddy water of the Big Warrior.

The boat tender rushed out and hooked a safety cable to the back bumper of the car which finally righted itself and sat still. Everyone in the car except Uncle James was in a state of near hysterics. "Pet, you damned near ruined my shoe stomping on it like that," he said as he untangled himself from the maze of feet and legs on the floorboard.

Mama, still hugging the baby close to her bosom, slumped back in the seat and moaned, "Oh, Lord, if you'll just get me back home, I promise you I won't ever attend another wake until it's my time."

Chapter Two

If the troubles of the world seem to bother you so
And burdens seem to get you down;
If your heart is heavy and your feet get slow
And all you want to do is frown;
I can tell you of a cure and it doesn't cost much,
A price anybody can afford;
All you got to do, brother, I'm telling you,
Is come a little closer to the Lord.

CHARLES (RUSTY) GOODMAN

Winter came early, and hunger rode the winds over the red clay hills of Alabama. Cold weather had set in with a killing frost. The last of the leaves had fallen from the bare trees, and only the pines stood clothed, black and cold against the pale skies.

Mama stood at the window of the old house on the outskirts of Birmingham in the East Lake section. She was waiting for Uncle Herschel Nix, her brother-in-law, to arrive to help us with the moving.

The door to the house banged open, and daddy stepped inside, his face blue with cold and his eyes watering from the chilling wind that swept down from the Appalachian hillsides. "Herschel ought to be here pretty soon," he wheezed as he rubbed his hands together. "You got everything ready?"

The pile of old clothes and few sticks of furniture in the middle of the floor of the two-room shanty represented all our earthly possessions. Daddy had moved a few big pieces the week before and then asked Uncle Herschel to take a day off from the sawmill and come move the family with his old Model T touring car.

Ordinarily this would have been a big adventure for us except we all had the mumps. Even mama.

Daddy stood in the middle of the floor and looked us over as we sat huddled against the wall. I was sitting on the floor, and Ruth was in my lap, her little jaws poked out like a squirrel with a mouth full of walnuts. Gussie Mae, Stella Mae, and Eloise were sitting beside me, legs extended, leaning back against the bare wall. Daddy laughed, "You all look like a chipmunk convention."

"It's not funny," mama said through swollen cheeks. Her neck and face were badly puffed up, and she had been running a high fever. Besides that she had announced earlier that she was going to have another baby. But with work that needed to be done, Mama simply refused to go to bed.

Now we were having to move. We'd been through it many times before: the rent was three months past due, and daddy's pension check had been used to buy food. There wasn't any other income so we had no choice but to find another place to live.

"Sam, sometimes I just don't think it's worth it. All we've ever done is move. Samoset. Sipsey. Jasper. Dora. Birmingham. Saragossa. Cullman County. East Lake. And this time I don't even know where you're taking us."

"Bremen, mama," daddy said patiently. "I know it ain't much, but it's a little house down in the holler, and we'll have some fields we can grow vittles in, which is better than staying here and starving."

"I reckon so," mama sighed, looking over at us as we sat pitifully along the wall. "But I just don't know how much a body can stand."

Daddy reached over and put his long arm around her shoulder. Suddenly I was dramatically aware of the tremendous difference in their ages. Mama was only thirty-six, but she looked haggard, worn, and, even with swollen glands, her face seemed drawn. Daddy, in his sixties, had always looked old to me, even though he was strong as a bull. His huge arms drew mama clumsily against his chest, and they stood there together, looking out the window at the bleak countryside. Their bodies were framed in the window as they stood silently, listening to the sound of the chilly wind whistling through the cracks in the house and sweeping beneath the doorsill. The panes rattled with a monotonous tinkling sound, but there was a domestic warmth that filled that old house making everything seem all right.

Outside I heard the coughing and sputtering of the old open-top Model T as it made its way slowly around the bend in the rutted red road that was frozen to flintiness. We jumped to our feet, pulling our blankets and quilts around our shoulders, and rushed to the window just in time to see Uncle Herschel bounce to a stop in front of the house.

Moments later he was inside, his cheeks bright red from the sting of the freezing wind and his old cap pulled tightly down over his ears. He looked at us sitting on the bare floor and shook his head. "You load 'em up," he said to daddy, "and I'll put the rest of your stuff in the car."

Before long we were piled in the back of Uncle Herschel's open car. He stacked the old clothes and bits of furniture around our feet and in our laps, and daddy pulled the heavy quilts and blankets around our shoulders and over our heads. The bitter wind stung our eyes and noses and made the swelling in our jaws hurt more. Just before he got in beside mama, daddy picked up our big old rabbit hound that had crawled out from under the floor and plopped him in my lap. Daddy had threatened to leave him if he didn't come out from his hiding place before we left. Now the warmth of his body protected me against the icy wind.

It seemed we had been riding all day when Uncle Herschel finally turned the old car down the dirt road that wound back over Bug Tussle Mountain behind the little country store that made up the community of Bremen. Ten minutes later we rattled to a stop in front of what was to be our new home.

Daddy went into the old house and lit the fire he had prepared in the stove. Within moments thick smoke was pouring from the old stovepipe that poked its way through the tin roof.

The children began to rouse themselves from the piles of quilts and clothes in the back of the car, but mama just sat looking. It wasn't much of a house. A small creek ran between the roadbed and the front of the unpainted shack with its sagging front porch. The afternoon sun was streaming through the scraggly pines, and the smoke from the fire crowded thick and gray over the top of the stovepipe, drifting toward the field below in the heavy, still air. "Nobody's lived here for a couple of years," daddy said as he helped carry the girls across the creek, "so we got a mess of cleaning up to do. But old man John Hall who owns it said we could farm the fields if we wanted."

Mama hadn't moved from her seat in the old car. She just sat looking at the weather-beaten boards, the broken windowpanes, and the dirt yard that had grown high with patches of weeds and briars. Ice had formed on some of the brown stubble under the eaves of the house, and the front door hung askew on one hinge.

"Sam," she said, her voice barely audible through her swollen jaws and her breath making little puffs of fog as she talked. "I reckon you know this is where I'm gonna have my baby. So I'm depending on you to make everything right before it comes."

Daddy, who had finally carried the rest of the girls across the creek, gingerly walked the old plank back to where mama sat in the car. Her eyes were brimming with tears as he picked her up and carried her across the footplank. Lowering her gently to her feet on the crumbling front porch, he said, "Honey, I know we're dirt poor. Right now it doesn't seem like we got nothing. But we got each other. I already checked with Doc White up the road at Arkadelphia, and he'll tend you when the baby comes. Nothing's gonna happen to you. You can count on that."

Mama wrapped her arms around his neck and buried her swollen face in his jacket. The two of them pulled open the sagging door and walked inside.

The spring thaws had just begun, and the rains had turned the little creek in front of the house into a raging torrent. A few yellow jonquils were beginning to poke their heads out of the hard soil in the front yard and tiny buds were appearing on the dogwoods when the first signs appeared that mama was getting ready to have her baby.

"Willie Howard," daddy shouted at me. "You get on Old Black and run up to old man Hall's and get him to drive into Arkadelphia and fetch Doc White. I think we're getting ready to have a baby around here."

I had been playing in the front yard with the hound dog, but dropped my stick and ran around the house to the field where the two mules were pastured. Old Black was the meanest mule this side of Sand Mountain. He'd just as soon bite a hunk out of your hide as look at you. But at least he'd run. Old Red, the other mule, was so lazy and stubborn that even when daddy put a cocklebur under his tail he still wouldn't move.

I opened the gate and ran across the field to where Old Black was grazing under a giant oak that was just beginning to put out new buds. It had rained all the night before and the pasture was soggy. That made little difference to me, though, for I enjoyed the feeling of the soft ooze squishing between my bare toes. Grabbing Old Black by the rope halter, I jumped on his back.

"Giddy-up, mule!" I shouted. "Mama's getting ready to have a baby and we ain't got no time to waste."

Old Black began to run. Round and round the pasture, missing the gate on the first two tries and finally bolting through and out on the road. But he took off in the wrong direction, back toward Bremen. I was hanging on for dear life and eventually got hold of his long ears and yanked his head around until he was pointed in the right direction. Then I let him run. Down the old, brown mud road into the hollow, past the soggy fields that still gave evidence of last year's cultivation, then up the side of the mountain toward the Big Road where old man Hall lived. It was about five miles from his place into Arkadelphia where Doc White had an office of sorts.

I slid off Old Black's back as we skidded to a stop in the Halls' yard and ran to the back door, pounding furiously and shouting, "Mama's gonna have a baby! Mama's gonna have a baby! Go fetch Doc White quick!"

Moments later Mr. Hall was out in the drive, cranking his car by hand and heading down the road for the doctor. I turned to see about Old Black, but it was too late. Mr. Hall's backfiring car had scared him off and all I could see was that mule, with tail flying high, running lickety-split back down the road toward home. It was a long walk back to the house in the mud for me.

Doc White arrived just moments before the baby. We heard his old car coming down the road, rattling and bouncing in the muddy ruts. Over the clatter of the car we heard something else. Doc was singing at the top of his voice.

Daddy ran to the door and stood looking down the road as the car slid around the bend and clattered into view. "Oh, Lord," daddy groaned as he leaned against the sill, "he's drunk again and just when we need him most."

The old car bounced toward the front of the house with Doc White sitting behind the wheel hanging on for dear life. His eyes were fixed straight ahead with a glassy stare, and the car weaved all over the road as Doc's voice roared out above the noise with the strains of "There is a tavern in the town, in the tooowwwnnn . . ."

Suddenly realizing where he was, Doc tried to swerve the car and negotiate the handmade bridge that daddy had built across the stream in front of the house. His judgment was off about four feet, and while he got his right wheels on the bridge, the left wheels slipped into the madly churning little creek. We watched in horror as the old open-topped car, with Doc White still hanging onto the steering wheel, slowly turned on its side in the stream.

Fortunately, he turned over on the upstream side of the bridge, and the force of the water kept him in the car until we could haul him to safety.

As we pulled him up the bank, we heard daddy shouting from

the bedroom, "Wring him out and get him in here. Mama can't wait much longer."

"Children, I sure am glad to see you." Doc White bellowed with a drunken slur. "If there's one thing I love in the world, it's children. Now you have called on me to bring another one into the world." He was shouting with dramatic gestures. "The miracle of birth is the greatest of all miracles and today we are about to witness . . ."

"Willie!" daddy bellowed from inside the house. "Get that old sot in here. This it it!!"

I grabbed the doctor by the arm and propelled him toward the door. Daddy bounded out of the bedroom and pulled him inside. I could hear mama moaning and crying from the bed. She opened her eyes and raised her head. Doc White stood at the foot of the bed, his hair down in his eyes, his clothes soaked with creek water, and his glassy eyes trying to focus as he weaved back and forth. Mama let out a horrible shriek as she saw him, and daddy moved to close the door so the children wouldn't be witness to what was taking place. "He'll kill me for sure," mama moaned as the door closed.

The four girls and I sat quietly on the front porch, looking at the old car on its side in the creek. We waited. The faint chirp of a spring robin was heard above the sound of the rushing water in the stream. A warm breeze stirred in the trees. Eloise, who was only five years old, was sitting beside me on the porch swinging her bare feet alongside mine. "Willie," she said innocently, "where do babies come from anyhow?"

Gussie Mae, sitting at the end of the porch, began to giggle. "Go on, Willie," she said, "tell her where they come from."

I stammered for some kind of answer. We knew that mama and daddy were expecting a child. We had heard them talk about it. But no one had ever told us where the baby was going to come from or how it was going to get here. "I thought the doctor was going to bring it," Eloise said, looking at me from under the curly bangs. "You reckon we oughta go look in that old car out there in the branch and see if he forgot and left it under the seat?"

Gussie Mae was laughing again. "He left something under the seat, sure enough, but it ain't no baby."

Just then the stillness of the spring afternoon was broken by a wail. We all gasped and listened as we heard it again—the faint sounds of a baby crying.

"It's here! It's here!" Eloise shouted as she jumped off the porch and stood facing us. "I hear it. I hear it. It's in the wood-pile behind the house. That's where it is."

Not waiting for us to answer she took off around the corner of the house as fast as she could run, her feet flying and little legs churning. The rest of us sat there for a moment, just looking at each other. Then, as if by signal, we all jumped off the porch and followed Eloise around the corner of the house, running as fast as we could. We knew there wasn't any baby in the wood-pile. But just in case there was—we weren't going to be left out.

It was half an hour later when daddy finally came to the back door and called us in. Doc White was sitting on a split log bench at the table, drinking coffee from a tin cup. His clothes had nearly dried, and the experience of delivering a baby had just about sobered him up. Daddy was grinning. "Come in, kids, and meet your new baby brother."

Quietly, solemnly, the girls fell in step behind me. Daddy opened the door to the bedroom and motioned us inside. We slipped through the door and stood around the foot of the old, iron, poster bed with the straw mattress and looked at mama. Her face was relaxed, the lines under her eyes and mouth were gone. I thought she looked beautiful. Snuggled on the pillow beside her was the tiniest, reddest baby I'd ever seen. She motioned for us to come closer. The tiny baby yawned and waved his little fist in the air, rubbing it across his tightly closed eyes.

"Boy," Gussie Mae whispered reverently, "he wasn't in the woodpile after all. He was right here."

We stood in silence for a long time, peering intently at the little bundle that nuzzled against mama's neck.

Doc White had gotten up from the table and came to the

door of the bedroom. Leaning against the doorsill, his coffee cup in his hand, he said, "He's a fine, healthy baby. What you gonna call him?"

Mama looked up at daddy with just a trace of a smile on her face, her eyes sparkling as she searched his face. "His name will be Sam."

Daddy grinned, and putting his long arms around the rest of us, he reached over and gently kissed mama on the forehead. "That's got a good sound to it," he said. "I know he'll grow up to be as fine a man as his pa."

Chapter Three

I walked with God thru all the years,
Thru flame and flood, thru pain and tears;
I'll follow Him, His voice obey,
I'm nearer home than I was yesterday.

—J. S. EASTMAN
Willis Publications, Inc.

By the end of the summer, daddy had really fixed up the old place. We didn't have running water, but there was a good spring right below the barn. It never occurred to us that it wasn't healthy to have the barn located on a hillside over the spring, although there were times (especially after a hard rain) when I thought the water tasted a bit strong.

That summer daddy finally got most of the twenty acres of bottom land under cultivation. We raised lots of green vegetables, some corn, and cane. Mama canned everything that could be canned, but it was the sorghum molasses that we liked the best.

That fall I worked with Gussie Mae and Stella in the fields after school, stripping the cane with a thin wooden paddle. Daddy came along behind us, whacking the stalks off with a sharp hoe and throwing them in the old wagon we'd bought from a neighbor. Daddy had worked out a deal with Mose Summey who owned the cane mill. Mose was letting us use his mill to grind our cane while he used Old Black to work the mill. This worked fine since we still had Old Red to pull the wagon in the field.

After the juice was extracted from the cane, it was boiled down into thick syrup and made into molasses. If we were lucky, we could sell it for a dollar a bucket at one of the country stores or swap it for a pound of lard or some seed. Mostly though, we ate it. Our diet consisted chiefly of cornbread and molasses, cow butter, field peas, turnip greens, collards, and buttermilk. We seldom had any meat on the table, but we grew healthy and strong on the potlikker even if we did stay hungry most of the time.

It was late one afternoon after we had been to Bremen trying to swap some molasses for fat back that the mules ran away. I had suspected that Old Black had built up a grudge against us because we let Mose use him at the cane mill. If there's one thing a runnin' mule can't stand, it's being hitched to a cane mill and made to walk round and round while the women boil the molasses and the men alternate between feeding the cane into the grinder and laying over to one side drinking moonshine.

This particular afternoon Old Black had been meaner than usual. In fact, he had bitten Zeb Tanner at the country store when he came out to look at the molasses in the wagon. Mr. Tanner got so mad he refused to swap the fat back we needed. I can't say I blamed him. Daddy was pretty upset and gave Old Black a mighty whack on the flank which didn't help his disposition a bit because right away he tried to bite daddy. When he couldn't get hold of daddy, he turned to Old Red and bit him. It's a good thing Old Red was as stupid as he was, or we'd have had one whale of a mule fight right there in front of the general store.

It looked like the afternoon was pretty well wasted. Mr. Tanner gave daddy a cussing out and stomped back inside the store. It was too late to try another store, so we climbed on the wagon and headed back over Bug Tussle Mountain toward home.

We had just started up the mountain when Old Black began to act funny. He kept turning around in his harness and looking at daddy—mean like. Daddy wasn't in any mood to be insulted by a mule giving him the evil eye, so he whacked Old Black on the rump with a stick and told him to mind his own business.

That did it. Old Black began to kick up his heels and before we could stop him, he began to run. Of course, Old Red, who had been pulling peacefully alongside him, had no choice but to run too. There we were, with a wagon full of sorghum molasses and two runaway mules—running up the mountain. It was incredible! I'd never heard of a mule running away with a wagon—*uphill*. But Old Black wasn't an ordinary kind of mule.

Daddy was pulling back on the lines and shouting at the top of his voice, "Whoa! Whoa!" The buckets of molasses in the back were slopping all over each other, and a couple of lard cans full of the sticky syrup had overturned and spread their goo all over the wagon bed.

"Get on the brake, Willie," daddy shouted. "Pull it back."

I grabbed the brake handle beside me and pulled it back all the way. The chocks rubbed tightly against the metal rims, and the back wheels locked into place. I couldn't believe it. The wagon, instead of slowing down, actually seemed to be picking up speed. The back wheels were standing still and were skidding along the bumpy road. Daddy was standing up and pulling back on the reins with all his might, and still those mules were just flying up the mountain pulling the wagon behind them.

"If they ever reach the crest of the hill and start down, we're goners," daddy shouted. But just as we approached the top of the mountain, the traces gave way. Both mules broke free from the careening wagon and bounded on down the road, still harnessed together, but kicking their heels and braying loudly— heading for home. The old wagon skidded to a stop just inches from the edge of the gully.

Daddy dropped his head into his hands and just sat there— shaking. Finally he turned to me and said, "That just shows you, Willie, a mean mule never forgives. Don't you ever forget that."

Daddy was right. I learned another lesson that year too. No mule is a match for a mad woman.

It was in December and daddy's pension check arrived the first of the month. As usual we were going to ride into Cullman to spend it on groceries and supplies. Daddy hitched Old Black and Old Red to the big wagon, and we began the sixteen mile drive into town.

It was a cold, icy morning and the ground was hard. The trees were standing bleak against the gray sky. The mules were too cold to give us much trouble, even when we rode through the old covered bridge that spanned the river between Bremen and Cullman. This was always a good place to expect trouble from Old Black because the sound of his hoofs on the wooden planks echoed off the walls and often caused him to rear up or try to run. We passed through safely, but I was so cold that I got off the wagon several times and ran alongside just to keep my feet warm. There was ice on the hillsides and in the puddles in the ruts of the road.

Rolling into town we pulled up by an old feed mill near the railroad tracks. I got out to hitch the mules so we could walk on up to the general store and trade with old Mr. Hunnicut.

Just as I reached for the reins, a switch engine, clattering down the tracks pushing two coal cars onto a siding, cut loose with a blast of steam. Old Black and Old Red had never seen a train engine before. They reared up, yanking the reins out of my hands, and began to bray loudly and at the top of their lungs.

"Steady boys. Steady!" daddy shouted. He might as well have been shouting at a waterfall trying to stop it from flowing. The mules kept on rearing, throwing their heads back and braying loudly.

Mama was sitting on the front seat in her best go-to-town dress, holding the baby in her lap. The wagon was jerking back and forth. Mama started screaming and the other children were in the back holding on to the sides and shouting for help. A large crowd of Saturday afternoon loafers gathered along the street and sidewalk enjoying the show. The harder they laughed the more excited the mules became. The entire street was in an uproar. To top it all, the engineer on the switch engine, seeing what was happening, blew his whistle loudly.

That did it. The mules began to kick and the wagon was shaking and bucking so hard that the tailgate fell open and little Ruth rolled out on the ground. Mama had a way of forgetting her fear when she thought one of her own was in danger. She handed Sam to Gussie Mae, jumped off the bucking wagon, and grabbed Ruth off the ground. Seeing she was not hurt, only scared, mama marched around to the front of the wagon shaking her finger at the mules and preaching to them.

"You ornery mules!" she screamed. "Stop that this second. Do you hear me? Stop it, I say, or you'll get the beating of your lives."

Well, nobody, even Old Black, could stand up under mama's tongue-lashing. Those mules just looked at each other in surprise, stopped their bucking and braying, and stood quietly in their traces.

One of the town bums, who had been laughing at the spectacle of a wagonload of country bumpkins about to be spilled out in the street, shouted, "That's the way, lady. Show 'em who's boss around your house."

In a flash mama turned on the crowd of loafers. "I'll show you who's boss, you bunch of good-for-nothing, tobacco-chewing, whiskey-drinking bums," she bellowed.

They scattered. I've never seen so many men run so fast in all my life. In moments the street was completely deserted.

Now mama turned and headed toward the switch engine. I guess she figured if she could back down two ornery mules and stand off a street full of Saturday loafers, she could whip a switch engine too.

Daddy stood up in the wagon and started to call to her. "Now, mama, don't do anything foolish."

But mama had her mind set on justice and wasn't going to be satisfied until she had an eye for an eye and a tooth for a tooth. The engineer, who had been watching from the comparative safety of his locomotive cab, saw her coming. Throwing the engine in reverse he pushed the throttle, and the giant wheels began to spin on the cold steel rails while mama descended on him like a chicken hawk on a biddy. Desperately the engineer pulled the cord that dropped sand on the rails. The madly spinning wheels finally caught and the engine lurched backward down the track just as mama reached for the ladder up to the cab. That was the last trouble we ever had with a switch engine, sidewalk bums, or even those mules as long as we lived in Bremen.

We had plenty of trouble in other ways, though, mostly from old man Hall and his son Amos.

Old man Hall was almost eighty years old and had the shakes. He wasn't able to hold still, even for a minute. He and Amos lived in the big house on top of the hill. Amos couldn't drive but the old man had a two-door, hardtop Model T that he cranked by himself and drove into town every Saturday.

It was in the early spring of the next year, when Sam was a year old, that old man Hall agreed to take us all into Cullman. It was the first of the month and daddy's check had arrived. Daddy needed to stay home and plant the garden, so Mr. Hall said he'd take mama and the children into town to buy supplies.

The Model T pulled up in the yard with the old man at the wheel. Children, chickens, and pigs scattered in all directions, and the two dogs set up a terrible barking. The car finally stopped and all seven of us squeezed in. We chugged out on the road, backfiring and jerking, and headed north toward Cullman.

To get out of the hollow you had to climb Bug Tussle Mountain which was no easy feat for a car of this vintage—especially when filled to overflowing with Goodmans. He got a good running start and lining up with a set of ruts started up the steep hillside. The car was straining and backfiring, and just as we reached the top of the hill, the engine choked and began to die. Old man Hall was shaking especially bad that morning and tried to get his hands to the hand throttle. Instead he hit the spark level and killed the motor completely. The car began to roll backwards.

There we went again, an old wreck of a car full of screaming

Goodmans flying uncontrollably down the mountainside. We were thankful for the deep ruts which kept us in the road, but when we reached the sharp bend at the foot of the mountain, the ruts held the wheels and the car tipped over.

Fortunately we were packed in so tightly that no one was hurt. Everyone in the back seat was hopelessly tangled together in a mass of arms and legs. Old man Hall, sitting on his head behind the steering wheel, was trying to untangle his watch chain from his long, white, handlebar mustache.

Mama was the only one with any presence of mind. Clutching the baby, she began a roll call to see if anyone was hurt. "Stella," she said, "squeeze through the window and run get daddy."

Daddy was in the backyard working in the garden when Stella came panting around the corner of the house. "Daddy! Daddy!" she screamed. "We've had a wreck. We all turned over, but no one was hurt."

By the time daddy arrived on Old Black we'd managed to crawl out of the overturned car. Mama was sitting cross-legged in the ditch with Sam in her lap. Daddy hitched Old Black up to the car and pulled it right side up.

Old man Hall somehow seemed to feel that the Goodmans were to blame and wouldn't let mama or any of the children back in the car. Daddy hitched Old Black to the front bumper, and with Eloise and Ruth behind him on the mule and mama and the rest of the Goodmans following the car, he pulled the old Model T back up the road to the house.

Our relationship with the Halls deteriorated badly after that incident. Amos tried to make us pay for his father's car. It wasn't going to cost much, but of course we didn't have anything. This made Amos mad, and he let it be known in no uncertain terms that he wasn't going to rest until he "got us."

It didn't take him long. Papa had gotten about half a dozen little pigs from old man Hall several months earlier. He was raising them to butcher. Slaughtering time in the mountains was always a big affair. As soon as the weather got cold, the neighbors would get together and make an all-day affair of butchering hogs. Of course, they always hoped that the owner would give them a mess of chitlins, some souse, or maybe a hog's head. But we never got a chance to slaughter the pigs because a man came along and bought them on the hoof—for cash.

Cash was the one thing daddy couldn't keep. If he had it, he had to spend it—or give it away. It really didn't make much difference to him just as long as he got rid of it. So early the next morning he was getting ready to hitch up the mule and wagon and drive to Cullman to spend his money.

Daddy was out in the yard when a stranger pulled up in a car and introduced himself as the sheriff of Cullman County. When he learned daddy was going to town, he offered him a ride. Daddy told us he'd catch a ride home that evening. He didn't know the sheriff had other plans. As soon as they got to Cullman, daddy found himself in jail. The sheriff said that Amos Hall had signed a warrant, charging him with selling mortgaged property.

"I don't know what you're talking about," daddy hollered from behind bars. "What mortgaged property?"

"Well, Amos Hall says he had a mortgage on those pigs and you sold them without asking his permission."

Now daddy was usually pretty level-headed, although the older he grew the easier he lost his temper. I guess it's a good thing the sheriff told him after he was locked up because I don't think he could have restrained daddy, short of shooting him, if he hadn't.

The first thing we at home knew about it was when a fellow drove out to our place and told us daddy was in jail for stealing pigs. Now the sheriff of Cullman County had never met mama before, and after this encounter I think he hoped he'd never meet her again. Early the next morning she got us all out of bed, told us we'd just have to skip school, and piled us in the wagon. She personally hitched Old Black and Old Red to the wagon, and we started the long trip into town. Although she didn't say much, I could see her lips moving, her eyes were like narrow slits, and her jaw was as hard as bedrock. I had a feeling that if mama could whip two mules, a street full of bums, and a switch engine, that she wasn't going to be cowered by a small-town sheriff or the likes of Amos Hall.

Mama didn't even hesitate when she pulled into town. Parking the two mules right in front of the courthouse, she told us to stay in the wagon. Mama got out and walked boldly up the steps and through the double doors. We stayed in the wagon, looking fearfully at the horrible bars in the windows of the jailhouse next door and knowing that daddy was behind them—perhaps, we feared, forever.

I don't know what mama did in the courthouse. I do know that moments after she entered a man came flying out the door and ran next-door to the jail. Minutes later he returned with daddy marching fiercely behind him, breathing fire. Daddy marched right past the wagon where we were all sitting and never gave a sign of recognition. We could see by the set of his mouth and the glint in his eye that he was out for blood—probably Amos Hall's.

We were right. The first thing he did was take the money he received for selling the pigs and hired a lawyer to bring suit against Amos Hall.

I don't think anything ever came of it, although everyone seemed to be satisfied. Amos Hall had his pound of flesh. He'd not only had daddy locked up overnight but had scared the rest of us into thinking he was going to be in prison the rest of his life. And daddy had his satisfaction in filing a lawsuit against Amos Hall and causing him to have to spend considerable money defending himself. Of course, the lawyers were the happiest of all because they not only got Amos Hall's money, but they also got everything daddy had received for selling the pigs.

The only positive result of the whole affair was that daddy finally decided it was time to move on. Shortly afterwards we packed everything we had (including the old wood-burning stove) in the wagon and hauled it across the mountain to Vinemont, five miles north of Cullman and twenty miles from the Halls. It was there, for the first time in my life, I began to sense that God had a bigger plan for me than I'd ever realized before.

Chapter Four

The town of Vinemont was just a few stores, a school building, and some shanties. The little house we moved into was located on the side of a hill near the First Baptist Church. This made things convenient, because even though daddy didn't care much about going to church, mama thought it was time the rest of us started.

The thing that attracted me to the little frame church was the piano. I'd never seen a piano before, although shortly after we moved to Vinemont, daddy traded an old radio for an even older pump organ. Mama had learned how to play the pump organ as a child, for as mean as Grandpa Sargeant was, he still loved to sing and wanted his children to learn music. Everyone in the north Alabama hills, including daddy, had learned to sing the shaped notes of the old Sacred Harp school. We called it "fa-so-la" singing. I had heard mama play the pump organ and had heard grandpa singing "fa-so-la" as far back as I could remember.

I was twelve years old, and mama said this was the proper age to join the church. When I talked with Brother Lehman, the pastor, he warned me not to make such a move until I was "saved." I asked him what that meant, and he suggested I find out by attending a series of revival meetings that were being held that week.

A certain Sister Newman was preaching, and mama and I attended the meetings each night. There were some things that took place that I didn't understand. I found out later that most of the church leaders didn't understand them either.

One night during the revival some of the folks "fell out" under the power of God. It happened during the altar call while Sister Newman was praying. Several of the women collapsed on the floor. The men weren't able to revive them and finally had to haul them home in the back of a wagon.

"Mama," I asked on the way home, "what happened to those women who fell down?"

She hesitated and said, "I don't know, Willie. It sure was strange, wasn't it? I'm supposin' they were sick and fainted."

I accepted her answer, but the next night those same women were back and they sure didn't look sick to me. They were shouting and praising the Lord and they had a radiant look of joy on their faces. This time I kept my eyes open during the altar call and watched while Sister Newman prayed for the people who came forward. Many of them threw up their hands and with a shout fell backward to the floor.

Some of the deacons rushed forward, put smelling salts under the women's noses, and revived them. But when they came to, they jumped to their feet, dancing, shouting, and praising God. I looked up at mama. She was standing there with her mouth open. "I've never seen the like," she gasped, "and right here in the house of the Lord."

She grabbed me by the hand and pulled me out of the meeting. "Them ladies is plumb crazy. You'd never catch me dancing and shouting and acting like that in God's house."

It was at the close of the two-week revival that I finally learned what it was to be "saved." That night, for the very first time, I took a look at my spiritual condition and saw how empty and lost I really was. Tears flooded my eyes and ran down my face. I was sitting on one of the old benches near the back when Sister Newman gave the altar call. "Sinner!" she shouted. "All you have to do to get saved is give up and let Jesus take over."

It was as if someone had turned on a light in the darkness of my soul. That night a skinny little twelve-year-old boy got up from his seat and stumbled forward to the altar. There I asked God to forgive me and in my own childlike way, I accepted Jesus Christ as my personal Savior. It was the one act in my life that pointed me in a direction that would reap untold joy forever. Mama made a long white robe for me, and three weeks later I was baptized in the lake near Vinemont.

Every Sunday morning I was up early and climbed the hill to the church building before anyone else arrived. It wasn't Sunday school that attracted me, though; it was the piano. I wanted to get there first so I could sit on the piano bench and hit the keys one at a time, trying to pick out some of the old familiar tunes. I started with one finger playing "Nothing but the Blood of Jesus." Before long I had learned to add the alto and was playing it with two fingers.

Sister Lilly Bradshaw, who played the piano for the church services, had little patience with me. "That Goodman boy," I overheard her complaining to Brother Lehman one day, "is nothing but a pest. Ever since he joined the church he's been fooling around with this piano. Last Sunday we couldn't get him in his Sunday school class because he wanted to sit up here and pick at the keyboard. Now preacher, if you don't do something about it, I'm going to."

Either Brother Lehman didn't want to do anything about it, or if he did, he didn't do it soon enough—because the very next Sunday Sister Bradshaw did. I had arrived early and was sitting at the piano bench picking out a new tune with the index fingers of both hands. Suddenly and without warning the piano lid crashed down on my fingers. I yanked my hands out from under the heavy wooden lid and looked up to see Sister Bradshaw standing over me, sparks shooting from her eyes. "I told the preacher if he didn't make you stop messing around with my piano that I was going to. Now you get up from this bench right this minute and get out of here. Don't you ever touch that keyboard again."

My fingers were aching and bruised, but the deeper hurt was in my heart. "I'm sorry, Sister Bradshaw," I said nursing my hands, "but how'm I ever gonna learn to play unless I . . ."

She reached over and grabbed me by the ear, literally picking me up from the piano bench. "Don't you dare talk back to me, you little white trash. Learn indeed! The likes of you don't ever learn nothing. What makes you think you could ever learn to play the piano anyway? And even if you did, what would you do with it—play in some honky-tonk? You'll never amount to anything anyway so get out of here and don't come back."

I did come back though. Time and time again. The lid was slammed on my fingers many times after that, but deep inside something was telling me that I was born to play the piano— and no Sister Bradshaw was going to keep me from it.

It wasn't long after that while walking home from school I passed a house near the church building. Mrs. Nash, who attended the First Baptist Church, called to me in a weak voice from her front porch.

"Young man, come up here on the porch for a moment, will you?"

I turned and made my way up her walk. She came out on the steps. "Don't I see you at church?" she said, her voice quivering with age.

"Yes, ma'am."

"Aren't you the boy who's always up there playing around with the piano?"

"Well, uh, I guess so," I admitted hesitantly, afraid she was going to fuss at me.

"Have you ever had piano lessons?"

"No, ma'am," I answered politely. "But that don't make no difference. I figure I can teach myself if folks'll leave me be."

"I think you can, too," she said smiling sweetly. "And I admire your spirit."

"You do?"

"I certainly do," she continued. "Now I have an old piano here in my front room that my husband used to play before he died. I don't want to sell it because he loved it so, but it sure does need someone to play on it. Would you be interested?"

"Would I!" I exclaimed. I couldn't have been happier if she had offered me a white pony and a basket cart for my very own.

She smiled and said, "Well, why don't you come on in now and see if it fits your fingers. If it does, you can come by any time you want and play to your heart's content."

That night, lying on the old straw mattress on the floor beside the other children, I couldn't sleep. Different tunes kept running through my head and in my imagination I would pick them out with two fingers on a piano keyboard. How wonderful it must be, I thought, to be able to play with both hands and use all ten fingers. Will that day ever come, I wondered?

Later that year daddy's brother Uncle Ode came to live with us. His real name was Otis Goodman, but all us kids called him Uncle Ode. That was about the same time my brother Charles was born. We call him Rusty, but his real name is Charles. By then having babies had become second nature with mama.

We all loved Uncle Ode and accepted him as a member of the family even though he was an alcoholic. He was good to us kids, and the only harm he seemed to do by his drinking was to himself. It hadn't always been that way because Uncle Ode had harmed a lot of people with his drinking. He had divorced his wife and lost his home. Now, sick and broken-hearted, he had come to live with us because no one else would have him.

One night Uncle Ode was out with some of his cronies, and

on their way back home they stopped at the Woodmen of the World lodge and joined. At the same time he signed up for a two-thousand dollar life insurance policy.

The next day the head man of the WOW lodge came to see daddy. "Now, Mr. Goodman, Otis has taken out this policy, and I know he can't afford to keep it up. But he's going to die one of these days because a man can't drink as much moonshine as he does and still live. This is a good policy, and he's named you as the beneficiary. Why don't you just keep it up for him?"

It was a smart investment, even though it took every penny of his pension check to pay the rent and make the payments on the policy. For several months we didn't even have enough money to buy groceries. Fortunately, however, there was a grocer who was also a Woodman. He knew daddy was paying on the insurance policy, and he also knew that Uncle Ode didn't have much longer to live. So he gave us credit and we bought all our groceries for six months without cash—knowing that sooner or later we'd come into some money.

Uncle Ode died in the early fall of 1932 and shortly after we received a check for two thousand dollars. After living on daddy's fifty-dollars-a-month pension check all these years, two thousand dollars was more than we could imagine. We were rich.

Overnight our social status changed from being the poorest people in Vinemont to being the richest. Daddy marched down to the grocer and paid his bill. Then with a flourish he handed the grocer a fifty-dollar bonus.

That was where the trouble started. Mama hit the ceiling. "Sam Goodman," she shouted, "when God finished making all the fools in the world, he poured everything that was left over into one mold and made you. I've been pleading with you for months to save that money and buy that twenty-five-acre farm with the house on it. Now here you are doing what you've always done, giving your money away without spending a dime on your family."

Daddy and mama almost separated over that. When it came to his money, no one was going to tell daddy how to spend it.

He might have bought that farm if mama hadn't been so insistent. Instead he just closed his mind on the whole idea. It was his money, and he was going to spend it just the way he wanted to.

He did do one good thing, however. Even though daddy seldom went to church, he knew that I had been playing on the piano up there. He also knew that I had been stopping by Mrs. Nash's to play her piano. "'Taint right for the boy to have to play somebody else's piano," he told mama. "There's an old piano for sale down at the feed store for fifty dollars. I'm gonna get it for him so he'll have one of his own."

I went with daddy to get the piano that afternoon after school. On the way over, riding beside him on the seat of the wagon, I asked him what kind of piano it was. He grinned and said it was a "Beat Up" brand. I didn't know what kind that was but it sounded pretty important.

He backed the wagon up at the feed store while the men loaded the piano. "You'll have to get some of your folks to help you get it off, Mr. Goodman," they cautioned as he paid them. "It sure is heavy."

Just as we got to the outskirts of town, however, Old Black pulled one of his stunts and decided to run the rest of the way home. "Whoa, mule!" daddy shouted. But it was too late. The piano scooted backwards, knocked out the end of the wagon, and crashed on its back in a mud puddle in the middle of the road. I jumped clear but there was nothing I could do. The piano lid had come off and was on the other side of the road in a ditch, and the keyboard was covered with mud and dirt. Sitting down beside it I rested my head on the muddy keys and cried.

Daddy got the wagon turned around and some men came from nearby houses to help us put it back on the wagon. Daddy assured me that "Beat Up" brand pianos are the toughest kind in the world and the men standing around all nodded their heads knowingly. Even though the men volunteered to follow us home and help unload the piano, I was not to be consoled.

The piano was carefully unloaded at the house, and the men put it in the front room across from the old pump organ. Mama wiped off the caked mud and picked the dirt out of the keyboard. Then daddy put the top back on and with a flourish pulled out the piano stool, motioning for me to sit down. I looked around the room at mama and daddy, Gussie Mae, Stella, Eloise, Ruth, Sam, and Rusty. Every eye was on me. The men who had helped us carry the piano were standing in the door, grinning shyly. I took my seat and timidly reached out and put my fingers on the keys. It was one of the great moments of my life. Softly at first, then louder and with more confidence, I began playing with two fingers. First mama, then the girls, and finally daddy and the men joined in singing as I played: "What can wash away my sin? Nothing but the blood of Jesus. What can make me whole again? Nothing but the blood of Jesus . . ."

Early the next year we went to Birmingham and bought a car. "Money ain't gonna do a man any good sitting around in a sock drawer," daddy said. "I've always wanted to own a car and this'll probably be the only chance I'll ever get." It was a brand new, 1933, Chevrolet two-door sedan. We had shopped around and daddy thought this was the finest car in the country.

The rest of the insurance money didn't last very long. What daddy didn't waste, he gave away. Word came that Uncle Herschel and Aunt Flossie were having a hard time down in Dora. Late one afternoon daddy asked me to drive him down to see them. "Maybe we can help them out a bit," he said sincerely.

Uncle Herschel was working in a sawmill for Grandpa Sargeant. Times were hard, but even in good times grandpa never paid his workers very much . . . especially those who were kin to him. Even though Aunt Flossie was his own daughter, they were nearly starving to death while grandpa drove around in a Peerless with a chauffeur.

Things were in a terrible state. They had been out of food for two days, were dressed in rags, and didn't even have coal for the little iron stove that heated the shack where they lived.

Daddy and I went down to the company store and bought

them ten dollars worth of groceries. Then we took Aunt Flossie over to Warrior and daddy bought her a new dress, a new hat, and new shoes. It was an investment that Aunt Flossie would one day repay (although not in material things) a million fold.

Driving home that night daddy said very little, but I knew what he was thinking. He was thinking that this was just about the finest thing he'd ever done. I looked at him, his shaggy white head resting on his chest, his old straw hat pulled down over his eyes—and I felt proud to be his son.

In just a few months all the money was gone, and we were right back where we started. During this time we had moved into another house in Vinemont and the rent was higher, so when the money ran out we knew we would soon be moving again.

The only thing I hadn't counted on was losing the car. It seemed daddy had never gotten around to making any of the monthly payments. It was a sad day when they took the car away. Daddy wouldn't come out of the house, but all the children—Gussie Mae, Stella, Eloise, Ruth, Sam, Rusty, and I— stood on the front porch and watched with tear-filled eyes while the men from the mortgage company backed the car out of the yard and drove it back to Birmingham.

We had tasted success and it was sweet. But I had also come to realize that success is a fleeting thing, for the only things we salvaged out of all that money were the things we had given away. It was a lesson I would never forget.

Chapter Five

It's a wonderful feelin' when on your knees you're kneelin'
And you get saved—
You can tell the story of His savin' glory
When you get saved—
I thank Him every day for His love and favor
Just can't give enough praise to my Saviour,
It's a wonderful feelin' when on your knees you're kneelin'
*In prayer.**

—RUSTY GOODMAN

Daddy met old Doc Booth while we were still living in Vinemont. When he found out the doctor owned a big, empty house in Hartselle, he talked him into renting it to us for fifteen dollars a month. After packing our few belongings into the wagon, Old Black and Old Red pulled us north to Hartselle. We were back on starvation rations, but it was always a happy time when we moved into a new territory.

The big old house was on Barclay Street. It was a white, two-story, ante-bellum structure with fifteen rooms and a porch that wrapped all the way around the bottom floor. This was one of the few times we lived "in town," and we really enjoyed it.

Things were getting tough, however, all over the country. The depression had hit and some of the mines were closed down.

* "It's a Wonderful Feeling" by Rusty Goodman and Joe Poovey © 1965 Reico Music Publishers, Inc. Used with permission of the publisher; all rights reserved.

Besides that, Roosevelt had been elected president, and one of the first things he did was cut the Spanish-American War veteran's pension down to fifteen dollars a month. That meant everything we had went for rent. Dr. Booth finally agreed to let us have the house for nothing, just as long as we agreed to take care of it.

It wasn't long before we were deep in debt to the grocer. Because of daddy's small monthly pension we weren't eligible for relief. To pay the debt he finally took the milk cow down and gave it to the grocer. About the same time we lost our mules. Then Doc Booth was killed crossing the road between his house and a tavern, and we had no choice but to move— again.

When things get real rough, you want to be near your kinfolks, even if they are just as poor as you. Uncle Herschel came up from Burnwell and helped us move back to the little community of Dora. Starting out in Dora was like starting all over again. Every day was the verge of disaster. No food. No money. No means of support. If it hadn't been for gravy and lye soap, we'd have never survived. We did have two old scraggly hens that provided a few eggs for us, but we had moved so much that whenever an old truck or wagon backed into the yard, they lay down and stuck their feet in the air so you could tie their legs together.

We found an old field several miles from where Uncle Herschel and Aunt Flossie lived. I was thirteen years old and able to handle an axe and saw. And Uncle Herschel loaned us his mule. I cut down the pines, trimmed the branches off, and snaked them down the mountain behind the mule. Daddy notched the ends and built a crude log cabin in the clearing. The cabin wasn't much, but it was shelter. It was a long, shotgun type building with a lean-to on both ends. The bedroom was at one end and the kitchen was at the other. There was an open loft in the ceiling where some of the kids slept. We put mud between the logs to keep out the wind, and daddy found several old window frames for light. There was no need for ventilation—we had plenty of that.

The floor was packed dirt, and the roof was made from shingles riven out of pine logs. Even though it leaked in a heavy rain, we were thankful for shelter and protection from the cold.

Uncle Herschel and Aunt Flossie lived across the mountain at Burnwell Switch, which was where the trains switched tracks to go down to the mines. It was here that Aunt Flossie had her big experience with the Lord.

Aunt Flossie had always been a "good" woman. Her daddy had read the Bible to them every night (there was nothing else to do), and she loved Jesus. But even with this indoctrination she always felt there was more to the Christian life than simply being "saved." Knowing nothing about the power of God, she continued to try to live the "good" life, attend church, and show some evidences of holiness.

Uncle Herschel had gone to work in the Burnwell Mines. One afternoon before he got home from work, Aunt Flossie was sitting on the floor in their little slab cabin singing hymns out of an old hymn book. As she sang, she began to feel strange physical sensations in her body. Tingling. Shaking. She could feel the hair on the back of her neck rising, and her heart began to pound wildly. Fearful, she kept on singing, but the sensations grew more acute and suddenly she was bathed in great joy and happiness. Jumping to her feet she began to shout, "Hallelujah! Praise the Lord!" She found herself dancing around the room, shouting, singing, and overwhelmed with great joy and happiness. This lasted for almost an hour until she finally collapsed in a chair, exhausted and weak, but filled with a deep peace and joy.

When Uncle Herschel trudged in from work, his face soot black under the old coal miner's cap, Flossie grabbed him around the neck and told him about the beautiful experience she'd had. "It was as if God Himself came down and visited me," she cried, the feeling still with her. "All I've wanted to do ever since is praise God."

Uncle Herschel removed his cap, shook his head, and went

out to the well in the backyard. "It sounds to me like you've lost your mind," he said matter of factly.

But that wasn't the end of things. The next week a friend came by and asked Aunt Flossie if she'd like to attend a church meeting on Yerkwood Mountain, about five miles away. "They are meeting in an old house in the woods, and we can walk over after supper."

That night, after fixing Uncle Herschel's supper, Flossie and two of her friends walked the five miles from Burnwell to the old ramshackled house on Yerkwood Mountain. Most of the people had walked in from miles around. A young preacher from Georgia was preaching and singing. Flossie had not heard singing or preaching like she heard that night. The preacher said that in order to live victoriously you had to have an experience called the Holy Ghost baptism. This experience, he said, gave people great joy, freedom, peace, happiness, and love for their fellow-man. It was the same experience that happened to the disciples at Pentecost; only he said that such an experience was available today also. He then described how this experience was manifested—quoting from Acts 2 saying that they would speak in new tongues, they would shout and praise the Lord and even dance around the room. Flossie's heart leaped within her because this was the same experience that had been hers the week before. Jumping to her feet she testified of her experience and the folks gathered around her, shouting and praising the Lord. Later they laid hands on her for confirmation. After that, many others in the meeting cried out to God to be "filled with the Holy Ghost," and they began manifesting the "gifts of the Spirit."

It was after midnight when Flossie returned home and woke up Uncle Herschel. He mumbled that although he had doubts as to whether Flossie had lost her mind, these doubts were now gone. "You've gone stark, raving mad and will probably have to be locked up before the year is out," he said as he turned over and went back to sleep.

The meeting on Yerkwood Mountain continued night after night. Herschel was upset by Flossie's enthusiasm and some nights refused to let her go. But the meetings were gaining in enthusiasm and intensity, and word spread through the area that the power of God was falling on Yerkwood Mountain. "Those people act like they're drunk," an old mountaineer said after peeking in on one of the meetings. "They shout, run, dance, jump on furniture, even roll on the floor." Thus the name *Holy Roller* stuck across the years.

Finally one Saturday night Uncle Herschel agreed to attend the Holy Roller meeting. The next morning a cold winter wind was blowing stiffly and the scudding clouds overhead were deep gray. Flossie and Herschel left the warmth of their little slab house, crossed the icy creek, and started up the steep path on Yerkwood Mountain. Flossie, excited that Herschel was going with her, nevertheless harbored an inner fear that some of the manifestations would scare him away. He'd never heard anyone speak in tongues. He'd never seen anyone dance in the Spirit, and he'd never been around a group of people who hollered and praised the Lord in a loud voice. Still, the very fact that he was going stirred her heart, and she imagined she could see glimpses of sunlight through the overhead clouds.

"Looks like it may snow before the day's out," Herschel grumbled, helping Flossie over a log on the trail.

"Praise the Lord for that," Flossie said.

Herschel paused and looked at her. "Flossie, I just don't understand you. If it snows, I'll probably be out of work. We're hungry now. Yet you say 'Praise the Lord.' Now what kind of foolishness is that? I don't know what's come over you since you've been coming to these meetings."

"Well, once you get there you'll find out."

They walked in silence. The trees were decorated with sleet and ice, and the only sound was their own hard breathing or the occasional crack of a limb in the woods as it gave way to its icy burden. Hands were stuck deep in the pockets of their coats, and their collars were turned up against the biting wind. Herschel was walking ahead when he heard Flossie begin to giggle. Turning around he demanded, "Now what?"

"It's nothing," Flossie grinned. "I was just thinking what it was going to be like when the Holy Ghost gets hold of you. You might even become a preacher."

Herschel spat on the ground and grabbed Flossie by the wrist, yanking her forward as he strode off up the path. "Listen, woman, I may go to this crazy Holy Roller church with you, and I may have to put up with your fool babbling around the house, but one thing that ain't gonna happen to Herschel Nix is for him to become a preacher. Now I don't want to hear no more fool talk like that, ya hear?"

"I hear," Flossie said humbly as she stumbled along, trying to keep up with her husband. But her eyes were sparkling, and she had to close her lips tightly to keep from laughing out loud at the vision the Lord was giving her.

The meeting that morning was typical. As the intensity of the worship increased, some of the people began to shout. Others leaped from their seats and ran around the room. Some fell to the floor in great joy and rolled back and forth. So great was the activity that they knocked down the old stove pipe from the pot-bellied stove that sat in the front of the room. The young preacher, dancing in the Spirit, grabbed hold of the glowing red stove pipe and put it back into place. Uncle Herschel could hardly believe what he saw. He rushed forward and grabbed the man's hands, expecting them to be burned to the bone. But there was no sign of injury—they weren't even blistered. So great was his conviction that Herschel stumbled to the front of the room and collapsed at the little altar crying out to God. It was the beginning of a new life for Herschel Nix.

The young preacher moved on, but the experience of the Holy Ghost baptism remained—especially with Aunt Flossie. Along with this experience had come a new language—one that she didn't understand. When using this language as she praised God or as she prayed for someone else, wonderful things happened. Her new experiences also gave her a much needed emotional outlet. There was very little to be happy about in the coal mining region of north Alabama during the depression. Disease, poverty, starvation, death—all were part of everyday life. But through this new spiritual experience Flossie found a joy heretofore unknown. She was able to be sustained with joy while many around her were turning to sin, despair, or even suicide. No one could deny the great change that came in Flossie Nix as a result of being baptized in the Holy Spirit.

Two years later, after we moved into the area, Uncle George Williams came trudging across the mountains from the direction of Oneonta. Uncle George said that God told him a certain Flossie Nix had been baptized in the Holy Ghost and that God had directed him to search her out and start prayer meetings in her home.

Word spread quickly throughout the day that there was going to be a Holy Roller meeting at Flossie's home that night.

It was late evening as Uncle Herschel came home from the mine that he met a strange, old man walking along the road in the twilight. The man wore a black felt hat and carried a huge, black Bible under his arm. "I'm looking for the home of Flossie Nix," he said to Uncle Herschel. "Can you show me where it is?"

Herschel was puzzled, "Yes, I'm going there myself. I'll show you where it is."

Uncle George threw one hand in the air and said, "Praise the Lord, brother. I prayed God would send me to a man who knew the way." Looking closely at Herschel he squinted his eyes in the gathering dusk and asked, "Brother, have you been born again?"

Uncle Herschel, remembering his experience on Yerkwood Mountain, answered confidently, "Yes sir, I sure have."

"Hallelujah!" Uncle George shouted. "I knew God would send me to a born again man to lead me down the road."

Looking even closer at Herschel, he said, "Tell me, brother, now that you've been born again, have you been baptized with the Holy Ghost?"

Uncle Herschel answered forthrightly, "No, sir, but my wife has."

"That's good, but it ain't good enough," Uncle George replied as they walked along the dirt road. "Lot's of men are try-

ing to ride along on their wife's skirttails. It ain't enough for
your wife to be filled with the Holy Ghost—you gotta be too.
How come you're not?"

This kind of questioning appealed to Herschel Nix. He ap-
preciated people who spoke their mind, even when he didn't
agree. "Well, sir, I've been meaning to be filled with the Holy
Ghost, but there ain't been no one around to tell me how."

"Hallelujah!" shouted Uncle George as they turned up the
path to the small slab house on the side of the hill. "There's
sure someone around now to tell you how. My name's George
Williams, friend, and I've come to tell you how to receive the
Holy Ghost."

Herschel grinned as they climbed the steps. "And my name
is Herschel Nix and this is my home."

Uncle George began to dance on the steps. "Praise the Lord,"
he shouted. "You can trust God every time to send the right
person along. Brother, you may not have received the Holy
Ghost since you believed, but you ain't far from it. Let's get
started."

That night a great crowd of people gathered at the Nix home
for a prayer meeting. Uncle George couldn't read, even though
he carried his big Bible everywhere he went. Discovering that
Uncle Herschel could, he asked him to read the Scriptures at
the meeting. As the service progressed, the people began to sing
and finally began to dance. The little house, not made for forty
men and women dancing and stomping on the floor, began to
shudder and creak. Believing it was the Holy Ghost "shaking
the place wherein they gathered," the people increased their
tempo. They jumped up and down and fell on the floor until,
with a mighty shudder and horrible cracking, the old floor sills
broke. The rock foundation crumbled and the front room of the
house, filled with forty Holy Rollers, crashed to the ground.

It was after this meeting that the people decided they should
find a more substantial place to hold their worship services.
However, they didn't have to worry about upsetting Uncle
Herschel because that same night he received the baptism of
the Holy Ghost.

It was the next day that Uncle George Williams came to our house. He asked if I would be willing to help him build a tabernacle in the hollow down near the creek. I had dropped out of school to help mama and daddy raise the children and work in the fields, so I had time to help out. It didn't take long to hew out a rough tabernacle. It was put together without a single nail. Holes were bored, and Uncle George and Herschel used wooden pegs to hold the logs in place. We rived out shingles for the roof. They split logs and pegged them together for benches. A load of sawdust was brought in for the floor, and in a short time we were ready for our first revival meeting—a meeting that was to last every night for seven weeks.

Aunt Flossie invited us to attend the services. Daddy refused to go. "I may be poor, but I ain't no fool," he said. Mama and I attended the meetings, however. Even though mama still felt such shenanigans were strange, she could not deny the change she saw in people's lives—especially Aunt Flossie's.

It was late in the summer, 1934, when the Holy Spirit touched mama. It looked like it was going to be a scorcher of a day. The sky was cloudless, and the leaves hung motionless from the trees. After breakfast daddy had gone down in the field to weed the garden. Mama was sitting at the piano in the log cabin, her feet patting against the dirt floor as she played and sang softly. The children were playing around the door in the front yard, and I was helping Sam down out of the old dead tree at the corner of the house when I heard it happen.

Mama was singing:

> There's a train bound for glory,
> It may come most any day.
> If you want to go, if you want to go.
> Get your ticket and be ready for this train may come today,
> If you want to go, if you want to go.
> Get your ticket . . .

I wasn't paying much attention until mama got to the line, "Get your ticket." The power of God fell on her and she began to sing the line over and over. "Get your ticket, get your ticket, get your ticket . . ."

All of us realized something was happening. Sam, who was almost out of the tree, jumped the rest of the way to the ground and nearly knocked us down as we hurried to get inside. Mama was sitting on the piano stool. Her hands were no longer on the keyboard but were high in the air above her head. Her face was pointing up and radiated a heavenly glow. All the time she was laughing, crying, and shouting at the top of her voice, "Get your ticket, get your ticket, get your ticket . . ."

We were scared to death. "Go fetch daddy," I shouted.

Gussie Mae took off. Out the door, around the corner of the house, and down into the field. I sensed that whatever it was that was happening to mama came from God. The only person I knew who was acquainted with God enough to tell us what to do was Aunt Flossie. While Gussie Mae ran for daddy, I took off in the opposite direction, across the mountain, to get Aunt Flossie. Even as I crested the top of the mountain and started down the other side, I could hear mama laughing, praising the Lord, and shouting, "Get your ticket, get your ticket . . ."

Gussie Mae arrived with daddy first. He tried to calm mama, but she acted as if he weren't present. "Oh, Gussie," he moaned, holding her in his arms, "You've been such a good wife and now you've gone crazy."

Mama didn't seem to notice. She was too full of praise and joy.

I burst into Aunt Flossie's house and tried to explain what had happened. "She's just a-sittin' there at the piano laughing, crying, praising God, and shouting, 'Get your ticket.' "

"Well," Aunt Flossie said, snatching off her apron and grabbing a shawl, "I don't know what 'Get your ticket' means, but I sure do know what it means when a body starts laughing and crying and praising the Lord all at the same time. When the Holy Spirit falls, I want to be there. If you can keep up with me, Willie Howard, that's fine. But I ain't a-waitin' for you."

I don't know what the record time for cross-mountain run-

ning is in north Alabama, but whatever it is, Aunt Flossie broke
the record.

Mama had calmed down by the time Flossie arrived, and after
a brief time together Flossie left and went back to Uncle
George's. After telling him what had taken place, they knelt on
the floor to pray.

"Glory! I've just had a vision," Aunt Flossie shouted.

"Well, speak up child," Uncle George said, "tell me what it
was."

"I was caught up in the Spirit and saw Gussie Goodman coming through the woods in a white dress. She was coming to the
tabernacle to receive the baptism of the Holy Ghost. It was
wonderful. Hallelujah!"

That night daddy agreed to go with mama to the meeting at
the tabernacle. He still scoffed at spiritual things, but I think
he wanted to be close to mama in case she took off through the
woods at night hollering "Get your ticket." Daddy was dressed
and waiting in the front yard for mama. He had propped himself against an old wheelbarrow and was whittling on a stick.

"Mama," he called through the door, "I been waiting out here
half an hour. What's taking you so dadgum long in there?"

Mama couldn't decide which dress to wear. Daddy turned to
me. "Women! I don't understand none of them. Your mama
has tried on two different dresses and now she's in there putting
on a third one. It's a good thing the Lord ain't in no hurry 'cause
if He were He'd just have to wait for mama to get ready."

Having decided on the white dress, mama and daddy set off
through the woods to the tabernacle. It was already dark and
daddy was carrying a kerosene lantern. The rest of us fell in
step behind.

Aunt Flossie had arrived at the tabernacle early and shared
her vision with the assembled group of Christians. They all
began to pray. Several minutes later one of the men glanced
up and saw the light of a lantern coming through the woods.
Jumping to his feet he began to shout, "Look out there. Here
she comes."

The people jumped to their feet, and a great shout went up

as they ran into the woods to welcome mama and daddy. Poor
daddy. I guess he wanted to run for sure, but there wasn't any
place to go. He never did go inside; he just stood at the back of
the tabernacle under the overhang of the roof and watched.

It was 1:00 A.M. when mama finally surrendered and received
the Holy Spirit. She had gone forward during the altar call on
the pretext of praying for someone else. While she was there,
Uncle George said, "Sister Goodman, don't you want to receive
the Holy Ghost?"

Mama looked up at him and nodded. The people all crowded
around and laid on hands while Uncle George began to pray.
Suddenly there was a great shout. Mama straightened up and
fell backwards into the sawdust under the power of the Holy
Ghost. The people began to praise the Lord and sing while
mama spoke in tongues.

Sitting about halfway back between Ruth and Rusty, I looked
back over my shoulder at daddy, who was standing just behind
the back row of benches. His face was bathed in tears. One of
the sisters got up from the altar and tried to get him to come
forward. He just stood there, crying, and shaking his head.

It seems that the miracles were just beginning. Uncle George
had invited a friend of his, Amber Jax, to come preach at the
tabernacle. The meetings continued every night and large crowds
came from all the surrounding communities. Even daddy was
attending the meetings with some frequency.

However, whenever God's power is revealed, there are always
satanic forces that strive to divide and destroy. Such a force
appeared in the form of young Gordon Freeman. Gordon's sister
Isabel Crawford had been attending the revival meetings and
had received the baptism of the Holy Ghost. She had been
preaching to Gordon about his evil ways—especially about making moonshine. Gordon, thoroughly irritated, determined he
was going to put a stop to the happenings down at the tabernacle.

The night Amber Jax was to preach Gordon came to the
revival service. It was the middle of September, and the sun was

just setting behind the low mountains when he left his house with his cousin Victoria. Cutting through the woods toward the tabernacle, they passed an old woodpile near the path.

"Look at that," Gordon said, spotting movement among the logs. Grabbing a stick, he pushed away the stacked logs, and in the dusk of the evening he spotted a huge, fat copperhead snake, coiled and hissing.

"That's what I've been looking for," Gordon laughed. "I'm gonna catch that old devil and take him to the meeting tonight. We'll turn him loose and break up that revival for good."

"You ain't really, are you?" giggled Victoria.

"You just watch me. Izzie's been talking so pious about me needing the fear of God in my heart. Just wait till she sees this snake loose in the church. We'll see who's afraid then. He may even bite old Amber Jax. Haw! That'd really be something, wouldn't it?"

Gordon broke off a tree limb and with a deft movement of his knife cut the branches so they formed a Y fork at the end of the stick. Prodding at the deadly snake until he began to move forward, Gordon suddenly clamped the fork of the stick across the snake's neck, pinning him to the ground. The snake writhed and twitched in anger, his mouth open showing his fangs.

"Quick," Gordon shouted at Victoria, "fetch me that old coffee pot over there on the ground."

Victoria ran to the other side of the path and picked up the old blue and white speckled enamel pot with a hinged lid. Laying the pot on the ground, Gordon released the pressure on the stick and prodded the snake into the old, rusty container. When he closed the lid, Gordon said, "Victoria, gimme your belt off that dress so I can tie this thing shut. Then we're gonna go to church and have us a real time."

Victoria, relieved that the snake was finally in captivity, pulled off her cotton belt. Gordon tied the lid shut.

The revival service was already underway when Gordon and Victoria entered the rear of the crowded tabernacle and found seats about halfway down on the aisle. Amber Jax was at the pulpit, his Bible open and his hands raised as he preached. After listening for a few minutes, Gordon bent over stealthily and untied the belt that held the lid on the coffee pot. Suddenly jumping to his feet he shouted, "If you're God's people, let's see what you do with this here devil." He tossed the coffee pot out into the sawdust aisle, the lid flipped open and the deadly copperhead poked his head angrily out in the bright lights of the church service.

There was an outburst of screaming and carrying on. The inside of the coffee pot was dripping wet with venom where the snake, in blind fury, had struck at the metal sides. Now turned loose in the aisle, he hissed and wiggled his way out of the confines of the container. People jumped to the tops of the benches and climbed over each other as they scrambled out the sides of the open pavilion.

Gordon was laughing. "What's wrong, you all? How come yer feared of the snake?" I was standing with daddy at the back of the tabernacle in his favorite place, half in the light and half out. He grabbed his walking cane and stood his ground. "If that devil snake comes toward me or one of my kids, somebody's gonna have hell to pay."

But the snake never got a chance. Gordon's sister, Isabel, came flying down the aisle. "I'll stand up for my Lord," she shouted with determination. "I ain't a-feared of no devil." Reaching over, she gathered the hissing snake into her hands and held it over her head.

The people stood back in disbelief as Izzie began to dance under the power, whirling around as she prayed aloud in tongues. The snake grew meek. His hissing and striking stopped, and he lay calm in her hands, never attempting to bite her or even show any hostility.

Sister Izzie, still praising the Lord, finally got to the back of the tabernacle. Throwing the snake to the ground, she commanded it to return to the wood. The snake quickly slithered away into the night.

Suddenly our attention was attracted by another sound. It was Gordon Freeman who had flung himself on the altar and was weeping and crying in repentance. Many others followed suit, falling on their knees in the sawdust and raising their voices and hands to God in thanksgiving. No one left the tabernacle until the first rays of dawn brightened the eastern sky.

This was the first—and the last—instance of such an experience in the history of these people. Later on, cults of "snake handlers" grew up in certain parts of the country who made snake handling a test of faith. But as far as Pentecostals were concerned this was an isolated miracle that was never repeated. However, it did prove to the people that God was able to work miracles. From that time on no one doubted that the power of God was just as strong in 1934 as it was when the Apostle Paul picked up the poisonous snake on the island of Malta. Even though we knew we should never presume upon God by inviting trouble, the instance also proved the Word of God as recorded in Mark 16:17–18, "And these signs shall follow them that believe; In my name shall they cast out devils; they shall speak with new tongues; They shall take up serpents; and if they drink any deadly thing, it shall not hurt them; they shall lay hands on the sick, and they shall recover."

George Williams moved on shortly after this, feeling that he had completed his work in this area. As is often the case when a church is without a human leader, outsiders moved in and tried to lead the people away from the truth.

Three such teachers visited one night. "We heard Uncle George had been called away," one of the men said, "and the Lord told us to come over from Sumiton and share our knowledge of the Bible with you."

Glad to listen to anyone sent from God, the people allowed the three men to preach. The first doctrine they began to proclaim centered on Paul's command in Romans 16:16, to "salute one another with an holy kiss." This, they said, meant the men should kiss the women and the women kiss the men. In good Christian charity they said they were prepared to demonstrate how this should be done, regardless of how long it might take or how many demonstrations they had to give. In fact, they sug-

gested everyone immediately accept this long-overlooked com-
mandment and begin holding "holy kissing" services.

This was too much for Uncle Herschel. Even though he had
never taken part in the services except to read the Bible for
Uncle George, he could not stand by and let these lustful men
lead the people into carnality. Jumping to his feet he proceeded
to "rebuke" these teachers of false doctrine. He moved up and
down the aisle, his voice roaring like a lion as he denounced
sin and proclaimed the unsearchable riches of God.

It was his denouncing of sin—and the sinners—that stung the
three men the sharpest. He called on the Holy Spirit to cleanse
the people of God and to purge with burning fire these who proclaimed this false doctrine of the flesh.

One of the men, now furious with rage, jumped to his feet
and grabbed one of the flambeaus used to light the tabernacle.
The gallon jug was filled with kerosene and had a twisted rag
stuck in the top which burned with a lot of smoke and some
light. "The purge of flame is upon you, Herschel Nix," the man
shouted as he held the flaming jug directly under Uncle
Herschel's quivering, extended hand. Uncle Herschel never
flinched. His entire hand was engulfed with flames, but he
continued right on with his rapid denunciation of sin. For long
minutes the flames swirled around his hand but he was left
untouched, unburned. Finally, in exasperation the flustered man
lowered the flambeau and stood staring in fear and unbelief.

Suddenly Uncle Herschel came to himself. Realizing where
he was and what he was doing, he looked around at the startled
faces of his friends. Every eye was fixed on him. Embarrassed
and confused he rushed out of the tabernacle into the darkness and raced home through the woods.

It was midnight when he reached his house. Aunt Flossie had
stayed home that night with a sick child and heard him as he
entered the bedroom. He sat down heavily on the side of the
bed and began to cry. Flossie turned over sleepily and reached
out for his hand. "Honey, I'm afraid I've done made a fool of
myself at the meeting tonight," he said.

Aunt Flossie, now wide awake, listened intently as Herschel

related all that had taken place. He was ashamed of himself for having gotten to his feet, and the incident of the fire confused him even more. "I'm afraid I've spoiled everything. Not only did I disrupt the meeting but I may have ruined everything Uncle George started."

He paused, caught his breath, and continued with determination. "But I know I was right in what I done. Holy kissin' just ain't what those men said it was. I believe it's all right for the men to kiss the men (if they want) and for the women to kiss the women. But mixing it all up and going off into the woods to practice just don't sound very holy to me."

Flossie pulled her long nightgown about her and took Uncle Herschel by the arm. "The Good Book says that Jesus went into His temple and cast out those who had defiled it saying, 'My house is a house of prayer; but ye have made it a den of thieves.' God wants to keep His people pure, Herschel, and it sounds to me like He used you to help with that job. Let's go in the front room where we won't wake the babies, and we'll pray about it."

Herschel and Flossie went into the front room where they knelt on the floor—that same floor that once gave way under the stomping of the people of God. Herschel was still sobbing and Flossie began to pray. "Oh, God, if Herschel was wrong, then convict him of his sin and reveal your truth. But dear God, if he was right, then send your people to assure him."

As Flossie finished praying a great clamor was heard in the woods. It was the sound of many people coming up the path from the tabernacle. Peering through the curtains she saw the lights of dozens of pine torches and lanterns moving among the trees. "Either they've come to lynch you or to love you," Aunt Flossie said with some resignation. "Whatever it is, I guess I better get some more clothes on."

Uncle Herschel answered the rattling and pounding at the door. The porch was lighted with scores of people with torches. Others were pouring out of the woods and heading for the cabin. They forced their way inside and began dancing around the room, hugging Herschel and praising God in loud voices. "Hallelujah! Praise the Lord! Amen!" they shouted.

"W-w-w-what is all this?" Uncle Herschel asked.

"We met together after you left," one of them said. "We decided you was right in rebuking them false teachers from Sumiton. All they wanted to do was get our womenfolk out in the woods. We're behind you, Herschel, and we'uns think that God is calling you to be our pastor."

By this time Aunt Flossie was back in the room and was joining in the rejoicing. The room was so full there was hardly room to stand. Herschel, recovering from his shock and realizing this was the answer to Flossie's prayer, lost his shyness and began to shout. "It's a good thing I fixed this floor and put some extra rock under the sills, cause we're gonna have a real hallelujah meeting here tonight."

"Amen!" one old, grandmotherly looking woman shouted. "If David danced before the Lord, then so can I. Praise God!" With that she began to jump up and down, her feet doing a little jig while her hands waved joyfully in the air. Others followed suit and after that there was no stopping any of them. It was almost dawn when the last ones finally left to return home.

From that time on Uncle Herschel has been the recognized pastor of the church. He began preaching on a regular basis, first in the tabernacle, and later in a small log church which he helped build down the road.

Chapter Six

Thank God I am free, free, free
From this world of sin.
Washed in the blood of Jesus
Been born again.
Hallelujah! I'm saved, saved, saved
By His wonderful grace.
I'm so glad that I found out
He would bring me out
And show me the way.

James McFall

Even though grandpa was a Baptist, he really didn't believe much of anything. During the depression, while the rest of us were starving, grandpa would drive by in his big Peerless Eight with a chauffeur—but he never offered to help.

We were dirt poor, and hungry most of the time, but there was a new joy and happiness that filled every minute. Poverty had become a way of life. It was hard work, picking cotton in the sun, but we had to do it to eat. No one complained. We just thanked the Lord for our daily provision.

Times got harder. We couldn't afford to take our corn to the mill to have it ground into meal. Daddy took a nail and punched holes in an old piece of corrugated metal roofing to make a grater so mama could rub the corn back and forth to grind out meal. We existed on corn bread, turnip greens, field peas, and molasses.

Winters were the hardest times to stay alive. We didn't have

129

any heat in the cabin, but daddy found a big oil drum, fixed a grate in the bottom, and ran an old piece of stove pipe through the roof. We collected sticks and logs in the woods and sometimes found pieces of coal along the tracks.

The only social event in our lives was going to church. Uncle Herschel was preaching regularly at the tabernacle. Even though daddy was afraid of the Holy Ghost, he finally reached the point where he insisted we all go to church together.

It was five miles through the woods from our house to the tabernacle. On Sunday morning daddy's big rough hand would reach over and gently wake us. "Time to get up. Remember it takes an hour to walk to church and we don't want to be late."

We'd scurry around the house getting dressed. After eating dried corn pones for breakfast, we'd take off through the woods to Sunday school and church. Afterwards we'd wait to see if anyone was going to ask us to share Sunday dinner. If not, we'd sit around the tabernacle and worship the Lord. This would give me a chance to play the old piano, plunking away with two fingers. I still longed for the day when I could play with all fingers on both hands.

As the afternoon wore on and darkness began to fall, we could hear the old saints coming up out of the hills and hollows, shouting and singing. They would gather again in the tabernacle and worship until the early hours of the morning. When the service was over, daddy would carry little Rusty, who had gone to sleep on the sawdust floor, and we would start home through the dark woods. Mama would bring up the end of the line in case one of us fell down along the way. Church was all we had to live for and God was all that kept us going.

It was an early Sunday morning in April when Algy Nix, Uncle Herschel's oldest boy, pulled up in front of the house in a wagon. "Hey, Howard," he shouted, "y'all wanna ride to church?"

We didn't get many such offers. In fact, this was the first one we'd ever had. "We sure do," I shouted back. "We'll be out in a minute."

Sam burst out the door to be the first one aboard the wagon. Moments later he was back inside, laughing and panting. "Y'all get out there and see what Algy's got hitched to his wagon. It's a cow."

Sure enough, Algy had hitched an old steer to a flat bed wagon. "C'mon, climb aboard. Old Fred here can pull a wagon just as good as any mule."

Daddy stood in the door with his hands on his hips. "I don't believe it," he half grinned, half snorted. "I never seen the likes."

"Climb aboard and I'll have you to church in no time," Algy said. Rusty and Sam were already on the back of the wagon and the girls climbed aboard and sat with their legs hanging off the tailgate. Daddy and mama climbed up in the seat beside Algy, and I pulled myself up over the side and sat down beside Rusty.

Algy straightened up on the seat, clucked his mouth a few times, and wiggled the reins. That old steer let out a bellow and began to run. Now the trail into our clearing wasn't exactly a race track. In fact, it wasn't even a road. But that didn't make any difference to Fred. He was going full steam when he hit the first big rock in the road. Algy was hanging on for dear life and the wagon bounced high in the air. When it came down, all four girls fell off the back end. Mama screamed and papa grabbed for the reins but by then we had hit the second big rock. This time Rusty, Sam, and I bounced over the side into the tall weeds. We looked up just in time to see Fred drag the wagon over a fallen log in the trail. Mama, daddy, and Algy came off the seat and landed on their backs on each side of the road. Goodmans were scattered all up and down the trail.

Algy looked sheepish. "Grandpa told me he didn't think Fred would be much good hauling a load."

Daddy shook his head, wiping the blood and dirt from his face where he had fallen in a briar patch. "Well, son, that's one time that grandpa was dead right."

The Goodmans were considerably late for church that morning.

In spite of the hard knocks, mama never lost her faith. Daddy's faith was growing too, but like moss on the underside of a log, you sometimes had to turn him over for it to show.

It was in the middle of the winter that Ruth broke her arm. There was a light snow on the ground, and we were all huddled around the old barrel stove in the center of the room trying to keep warm. Ruth and Sam had crawled up in the open loft to play on the corn-shuck mattresses. They were jumping off an old trunk in the back of the loft and landing on the corn shucks.

One jump carried Ruth too far, and she fell over the side of the loft to the floor below. We heard her arm snap when she hit. Mama rushed to her and picked her up. She was unhurt except for the huge bulge on her left arm where it dangled limply from a break midway between elbow and wrist.

The only doctor was fifteen miles away. There was snow on the ground and we didn't even have a mule, much less a wagon. Ruth was screaming and the rest of us were scared to death. Mama turned and looked at daddy. "Sam, get down on your knees beside this child. We're gonna pray."

It was no time for objections. Daddy did as he was told and the rest of us followed suit. Ruth quieted down as she saw us kneeling in a circle around her on the old dirt floor. There was no time for introductions or nice words as mama began to pray. She started off shouting, beseeching the Lord to heal her child, rebuking the power of Satan and claiming the healing power of the Holy Spirit. The rest of us joined in, even daddy, praying as loudly and as earnestly as we knew how.

While mama prayed, she stroked Ruth's arm, pulling it gently back into place and holding it there so, as she said later, the Lord could "knit those bones together."

The Lord did just that. And he did it then. The prayer ended and Ruth's crying had stopped completely. Very slowly she began to move her arm, waiting for the pain to begin again.

There was no pain. Where once the bones had dangled loosely, now they were strong and firm. The arm was healed.

Music was still a big part of my life, even though I was not doing any more than singing the old hymns at church and playing the piano with two fingers. Daddy had picked up an old handcranked Victrola and somebody had given us some 78 rpm records of the McDonald Brothers Quartet. I was fascinated by the piano music. It never occurred to me that I should take piano lessons, but I just knew that there was music in my bones. At times I dreamed of sitting at the piano keyboard, running my fingers up and down the keys, and playing beautiful melodies. Yet, in the mornings when I climbed down out of the loft and sat on the piano stool, it was the same old two fingers painfully picking out the tunes that were in my heart.

I shared my dreams with mama who suggested that since the gifts of the Spirit could only be claimed by those who had been baptized in the Holy Ghost, that perhaps in order to claim the "gift of playing the piano" I should first receive the baptism. This made sense. Since I desperately wanted to be able to play the piano to serve the Lord, I began to seek the baptism of the Holy Ghost.

One Sunday morning, in Uncle Herschel's church, I stood to testify. Suddenly, a strange and wonderful feeling came over me, and before I knew it I was praising God in tongues. I was bathed in the same joy I had heard others talk about. After the service Uncle Herschel hugged me close to his chest and said, "You see, Howard, you don't have to find the Holy Ghost, He finds you." When I got home after the service I told mama what had happened. She began to shout. "Willie Howard, the Lord said, 'Ask and ye shall receive.' You asked and you've received. Now get in there and sit down at that piano and claim the gift the Good Lord has given you."

In my joy over receiving the Holy Spirit I had forgotten about the piano. I walked slowly to the piano stool and sat down. I looked at the keyboard and then looked at my fingers. Could it be possible that along with the baptism of the Holy Spirit the

Lord had given me the gift of playing the piano? Cautiously I
reached out with my two index fingers and began to play. While
I played, I prayed. Suddenly, like rivers of living waters, the
heavenly language began to flow just as it had in the church
house. My other fingers reached out, and as I praised the Lord
with great joy, I felt them falling upon those old worn, chipped,
cracked ivories. And there was music. It was music like I had
never heard before. My fingers were running up and down the
keyboard as I played "in the Spirit."

"Praise the Lord, it's mine," I shouted as my fingers played
the melodies that had so long been shut up in my heart.

And on the other side of the room I heard mama, her head
back and her hands up, shout, "Praise the Lord, it's his."

Chapter Seven

I've got up out of the bed many times in the midnight hour
To pray a prayer that it seemed no answer would come to;
Though I'd waited, patient and long,
But answers have come to enough of those prayers
To make me keep praying on.

It was time to move again. Despite our better relationship with the Lord, our relationship with the landlord remained the same. He wanted money and we didn't have any. Daddy learned of a vacant cabin up on Yerkwood Mountain, and in the summer of 1936 we vacated the old log cabin and moved.

There was a deep stream around the base of Yerkwood Mountain that had to be forded if we walked to church. Someone had bridged it with a footlog and stretched a piece of bailing wire between two trees to act as a hand support. After a heavy rain the log would be under water and we would have to feel our way along in the dark while the water raced past our knees.

One night Gussie Mae and I asked mama's youngest sister Cathryn to walk to church with us. We went by grandpa's to get her.

Grandpa met us at the door. "Awrrr, I'd just as soon she went to a dance as to a Holy Roller meeting." Cat, who was almost thirty years old, finally talked grandpa into letting her go with us.

While we were in church, there was a hard rain and the water in the creek rose over the banks. When we got back to grandpa's, Cat said, "Grandpa, Howard and Gussie want to spend the night. It's been raining something fierce and the water is up in the creek. They can't get across the footlog."

Grandpa was standing just inside the screen door looking at Gussie and me who were standing in the drizzling rain. "Well, this ain't no hotel, you know," he argued.

I grabbed Gussie by the arm. "C'mon, Sis, let's go. We'll just walk home."

Gussie Mae followed me down the trail. It was pitch black and the water was dripping off the trees. My old flashlight blinked off and on until we reached the creek, then it went off completely. We grabbed hold of the wire and started across, feeling our way on the log which was deep beneath the swirling water. Twice Gussie lost her footing and fell. She held onto the wire and I was able to pull her out of the powerful current. We finally made it to the other side, up the steep path on Yerkwood Mountain, and to the house.

The next time I saw grandpa he said, "Well, I see you didn't need to spend the night and mess up my bed after all, did you?" I didn't have the heart to tell him that Gussie almost drowned because of his stinginess.

I was seventeen when I started attending some of the "singings" in the area. Gussie Mae, Stella, and I made up the Goodman Trio. Whenever we heard a singing was to be held someplace, we'd walk across the mountains to the location. Perhaps it was a family reunion or maybe an annual church meeting. Since hunger was a way of life with us, we were always thankful when they served "dinner on the grounds." Sometimes we walked as far as twelve miles to attend a "singing."

It wasn't long before the Goodman Trio was known throughout the area. I attended singing school at the Doliska Baptist Church near Burnwell and later studied the A. J. Shorewalter rudiments, learning the lines and spaces and basic music composition. But I loved to sing more than I loved to study, so my formal education was limited to several weeks at the most.

Rusty was going to school at the little one-room building in Burnwell. Through his teacher, Mrs. Gurvis Brasfield, we came to know her husband, Aus. If it hadn't been for the Brasfields, we couldn't have made it that year. Rusty picked blackberries in the summer and put them in lard buckets to sell to Mrs. Brasfield. We found out later she didn't even like blackberries. In the fall of that year, 1937, we had to move again. Aus Brasfield, knowing of our plight, gave us an old house up at the mine where he worked. Sam, Rusty, and I, working side by side, tore the old house down piece by piece. Aus let us use his mule and daddy made a ground sled out of some old timbers. We loaded the lumber on that old sled and pulled it down the mountain. There, in a small clearing in the bottom, we put the house together again. Daddy planted some chinaberry trees out in the yard and we moved in.

Two months later mama had her last baby. Daddy, who was sixty-nine years old, picked the name—Bobby.

Chapter Eight

If you could own all the world and its money,
Build castles tall enough to reach the sky above;
If you could know everything there was to know about life's
*   game,*
Yet you've known nothing until you've known God and His
*   love.*

Until you've known the loving hand
That reaches down to a fallen man
And lifts him up from out of sin where he has trod;
Until you've known just how it feels
To know that God is really real;
Then you've known nothing until you've known the love of
*   God.*

—RUSTY GOODMAN

Daddy felt the time had come to leave Burnwell. Uncle Herschel agreed to move into our house and we made plans to move north to Cullman County.

It was at Cullman that I felt God calling me to preach. Stella and Eloise were now traveling with me in the trio and often, after we finished singing, I would be called on to preach. As the opportunities grew more frequent, I finally surrendered to the call and announced that I was available for revival meetings.

My first revival was at Carbon Hill, about fifteen miles west of Jasper, in early 1939. Stella and Eloise went with me. We sang, I preached, and we had a great revival. I came home glowing and gave the report to mama and daddy, telling them I had several other invitations and was going to start traveling and preaching. The very next day daddy went out and sold everything we had, traded our old Model A for a 1934 Pontiac, and announced that when the Lord called me He got an unexpected bargain for His money—because all the Goodmans were going to answer.

Gussie had married and left the family, which lightened the load somewhat. But still trying to crowd nine people (and some of us were pretty hefty) and all our luggage into a car meant to hold five persons was quite an accomplishment. Our first meeting was up in Winston County where we stayed with mama's Uncle Charlie Williams. I preached under a brush arbor. The meeting lasted three weeks, and the offerings were enough to help pay our transportation to our next preaching invitation—Mobile.

Foster Dismuke had invited me to come down and "run a meeting" for him. We arrived in the spring of the year and rented a four-room furnished house. The meeting lasted a month and then I preached at a Church of God in Crichton, just outside Mobile. That meeting lasted two weeks and then we didn't have any place else to go.

Mama was beginning to see the foolishness of daddy's plan to answer my call to preach. "It was bad enough being broke in Cullman County," she said, "but at least we had a cookstove and beds to sleep in. Now the rent is due and we don't know anyone to help us out."

In answer to her complaining daddy turned philosophical. "What do folks do when they're out of work?" he asked, not expecting an answer. "They either get a job or they hit the road. Now I'm too old to get a job so I'm suggesting we do a little traveling. I've always wanted to go to Florida. Let's drive down and see what things look like."

For lack of a better suggestion we packed our luggage in the trunk, strapped what was left on top of the car, and all nine of us started out for Tampa, more than six hundred miles away.

It was a mistake, just like a lot of other things we'd tried. Although in the beginning we could see the hand of God protecting us, we soon realized it was in spite of our decision and not because of it.

Leaving Mobile we got as far as the little town of Bonifay, Florida, where the old car sputtered to a stop right in the middle of town. We were out of gas, food, and money.

"You all wait right here," daddy said, climbing out of the car. "I'll be right back."

He walked off down the strange street and turned into a little furniture store at the end of the block. Moments later he was back, carrying a guitar. "I told the man we wanted to borrow it for a little singing," he said. Handing it to Sam who knew how to strum a few chords, he took off back down the street. Stopping at the end of the block he began to shout in a loud voice, "The Goodmans are gonna sing on this corner in a few minutes. Y'all come."

Within a few minutes a sizable crowd had gathered and we piled out of the car, stood on the street corner, and sang gospel songs. I preached a short message and then little Bobby took daddy's old straw hat and walked through the crowd taking up an offering. When we got back to the car, we could hardly believe our eyes. We had received eighteen dollars which was enough to buy us food and gas. When we pulled out of Bonifay, we had a warm feeling in our hearts, never dreaming that one day we would return as the featured singers in one of the biggest of all gospel concerts, the Bonifay Music Festival.

We never did get to Tampa. We ran out of gas and money again in a little town called Lutz. After sleeping in the car several nights, I was finally able to make contact with a Church of God preacher who let me preach in his church. The offerings were enough for us to rent a small cabin, and I began preaching in churches around the area.

Things were looking up until we began to run into a series of misfortunes. Sam had two serious bouts with pneumonia and without medical treatment mama feared his lungs would be scarred. Food was scarce and we were hungry all the time. And to top it all off, the old car broke down.

The garage man gave me a forty-dollar estimate for repairs, but when I went back to get it, he handed me a bill for one hundred forty dollars. "That old engine you had wasn't any good," he explained, "so I went ahead and put a new one in."

"But I don't have the money to pay for that."

"Then I'll just have to keep the car until you pay me," he said with a slight grin on his face.

And keep it he did. Had it not been for the help of Brother E. M. Ellis, the superintendent for the Church of God in that area, we would have never been able to pull through. However, he went on my note and we were able to buy another old car which provided some means of transportation.

"Maybe I'm just not called to preach," I confided in mama in one of my moods of depression. "It seems to me that if God really wanted me in the ministry, he'd make things easier. Instead everything seems to be going wrong. Maybe we ought to head back home and I'll get a job in the mines."

Mama looked at me with eyes brimming with tears. "Every mountain trail has rocks on the path to the summit," she said. "Those rocks can be blocks or they can be stepping stones. It ain't ever gonna be easy in the Lord's work, son. It wasn't easy for Stephen or Paul. And if you live for Jesus, it ain't gonna be easy for you either."

Mama paused, then looked me straight in the eye. "If Satan's making things rough, then you can bet you're doing God's will. The only time you oughta worry is when everything is going smooth. Maybe God is calling you to go back home. But it's not to work in no mine—it's to preach the unsearchable riches of the grace of God."

Our first stop in Alabama, after we got back, was Flat Creek. Here I met a preacher who invited me to hold a revival meeting for him. The church was small and poor, and they could hardly pay us anything. But it sure was good to get back among people we could trust. Our Florida excursion taught us something. Nothing can replace love and trust in people's hearts. Not wealth. Not prestige. Not even success in church and business. I determined I'd rather be poor all the rest of my life and love people than to be rich and not be able to love anyone.

Chapter Nine

I've trusted many a friend that's failed me
And left me to weep alone—
Ah, but I've found enough of those friends to be true blue,
To make me keep trusting on.

Loving people, I found, doesn't necessarily make them love you. We found this to be especially true in a little north Alabama community called Ford City.

The town had one major distinction—it was the bootleg capital of the state. White lightnin' was the community's major product—and drunken brawls, Saturday-night fistfights in the streets, gambling, and a murder every week were Ford City's major source of recreation. The hills around us were filled with stills which produced great quantities of moonshine, and all of them were guarded by rugged mountain sharpshooters armed with shotguns and rifles. Revenue officers had long since learned to stay away from Ford City if they wanted to remain alive.

We didn't know all this when we moved into the big old wooden house just outside the little community. Nor did we know the stigma that would be ours for just living in the house. The fourteen-room house was known as the Sherman Place, belonging to the granddaughter of a certain General Sherman. (We later discovered that one reason the house remained vacant was because of the unpopularity of its former owner, the same General Sherman who had "marched through Georgia.")

The big house was our headquarters. We went out almost

every day into surrounding communities singing or preaching in
the streets. If we didn't have an engagement, we would go down
to the crossroads at Ford City and I would preach on the corner.
My preaching was not the kind that won friends and influenced
people, although I could always get a good crowd because I
preached against moonshine, gambling, and immorality. The
crowd gathered as much to hear the audience reaction as they
did to hear me. Occasionally some mountaineer with a jug in
the crook of his arm would holler loudly, "You just keep it up,
fat boy, and you won't be long fer this world. One day you're
gonna wake up dead."

Whenever I preach there are people who disagree with my
message. Sometimes, in a street service, a drunk will stagger
to the front of the crowd and begin preaching in competition.
But the people in Ford City were different. They weren't just
fun-loving drunks—they were killers. The more I shouted
against the evils of moonshine and sin, the madder they got.
There was usually one murder a week, and it soon became
obvious that the Goodmans were next in line.

When Miss Sherman rented the house to us, she gave specific
instructions that one room was off limits. We were not to enter
it. It was an upstairs room without windows, and the door was
locked and bolted.

Now telling the Goodmans they can't go in a room is like
Br'er Rabbit telling Br'er Fox not to throw him in the briar
patch. It took us less than an hour to pick the locks and sneak
into that mysterious room just to find out what was there.

We found out. It was an arsenal. The room was filled with
muskets, rifles, shotguns, pistols, and enough ammunition to
hold off a small army. It wasn't long before we discovered we
would need it for just that.

The day before Halloween I went down to the crossroads to
preach. The drinking, gambling, and whoring were getting worse
every day, and I felt a strong compulsion to preach against them.
A good crowd gathered as the girls sang. About halfway through
my sermon a mean-looking man with a drooping black mustache stepped out of the crowd. He had a large lump on his

right hip under his coat. A brown stain of chewing tobacco juice ran from the side of his mouth. "I've had enough of you damned Goodmans," he shouted, his face livid with rage. "If you and those other crazies ain't outta town by tomorrow morning, we're gonna run you out. Is that clear?"

It sounded pretty clear to me. "That's tellin' 'em, Frank," voices from the crowd shouted. "Show 'em who's boss in this town."

The man with the mustache (whose name I took to be Frank) looked me straight in the eye. "Now we'uns mean business around here. Either you get out or we'll burn you out."

There was no sense continuing the meeting. I turned to the rest of the family and said, "We better head for home."

"Ain't you gonna take up an offering?" little Bobby shouted. But one look at the jeering, howling mob indicated that it wouldn't produce much yield.

That evening Sam and I drove into Sheffield to ask the sheriff for protection. "Son," he said, "you got yourself in that mess by preaching where you weren't wanted. Now you're gonna have to get yourself out. No man in his right mind would go down there and try to break up that mob. If I sent a deputy down, we'd find him next week, head down and full of holes in some old well. In fact, they'd probably kill me if I tried to recover his body. I'm sorry, boys, but if I were you I'd pack and run while you're still able."

Of course we didn't run. Our rent was paid up. Not even the threat of death could force the Goodmans to move while the rent was paid up. Besides that, Gussie and Stella and their husbands had moved in with us, and we had too many mouths to feed for us to leave without having any place to go. We decided to wait it out and see what happened.

It happened. The next night was Halloween. It seemed that everybody in town got drunk. We could hear them down the road at the two little stores and the filling station. They were drinking, hollering, and working themselves into a frenzy.

"Boys," daddy said as he came down the steps leaning heavily on his walking stick, "I think we better put out the lights and push some of this furniture up against the doors."

Daddy was approaching eighty, but it seemed the older he got the more he was "spoiling for a fight." Tonight it looked like he was going to get his wish.

We put out the lights and waited behind the barred doors. Outside we could hear the crickets and tree frogs in the big cedars that encircled the house. The sound of the mob far down the road had subsided, and we hoped they had gotten drunk and gone home to sleep it off.

Suddenly it happened. There was a terrific explosion on the front porch followed by wild laughter and the sound of running feet in the driveway. Another explosion occurred on the back porch. Three cars full of men pulled up in front of the house, hollering and shouting. We could see them piling out and running in all directions through the dark trees that surrounded the house. They were lighting firecrackers, throwing them on the porch and through the windows. They weren't regular firecrackers, but big, red cherry bombs that sounded like dynamite.

My mind was full of stories daddy had told me when I was a little boy. One particular story stuck in my mind. It was about a man in north Alabama who had promised to marry a girl and then backed down. The girl's brothers and their friends caught him in the center of town one Saturday afternoon. After beating him nearly to death with their fists, they ripped off all his clothes. Smearing his skin with melted tar, they rolled him in chicken feathers, tied him backwards on his mule, and ran him out of town. They finished the afternoon's entertainment by burning his house and killing his dog and chickens.

Stories like this rushed to my mind as I saw the mob of men running around the house, dodging through the trees and throwing their cherry bombs.

"Get outta town, Goodmans!" they shouted as they ran back and forth through the trees. "We're gonna burn you down, preacher."

"All right, boys," daddy said, pounding his stick on the floor. "Let's load up and show those buzzards a thing or two. If Teddy

Roosevelt could do it on San Juan Hill, so can we." He pointed up the stairs with his cane and we knew what he was talking about.

Moments later we were all flying up the steps toward that mysterious room with the bolted door. We had no time to pick the lock. I hit the door running at full speed and it splintered on its hinges and crashed down in front of me. The other members of the family scrambled inside, grabbing up guns and handfuls of ammunition. "No rifles," I shouted. "We might kill somebody. Stick to shotguns and birdshot. Then if they get killed it's their fault."

We fanned out through the upstairs. Everyone had a shotgun loaded with birdshot. We crouched below the window sills and waited. Suddenly I saw the light of a match in the cedars as one of the men lit a cherry bomb. Rising up over the window sill, I took quick aim on the tiny spark of light and fired. There were loud screams of pain.

"Praise the Lord," mama shouted triumphantly from the back of the room. "You got him."

"Hey," a drunken shout came from the side of the yard, "They's got guns up there. Let's burn 'em out."

I saw a match light from where the voice came from and looked around just in time to see Ruth poke her big, old twelve-gauge shotgun over the window sill and cut loose. The blast knocked her back into the room on her backside, but the cry of pain from the edge of the trees proved her aim had been true.

Then all bedlam broke loose. Every time we saw a flame there was the boom of a shotgun, usually followed by a scream of pain and sometimes by the sound of running feet.

"Whoopee," shouted Sam, running from one window to another. "Here's another one out here." We could see their dark figures darting in and out among the trees.

I suddenly realized I hadn't seen daddy in some time. "Hey, where's daddy?" I shouted. We began to panic.

"Maybe they've sneaked in and grabbed him. They'll kill him for sure," Stella cried.

Peering cautiously out the windows we saw him. He had

eased out the back door with a huge, long-barreled pistol and was cautiously making his way between the cedar trees, gun in one hand and walking cane in the other, stalking a shadowy figure standing behind a large tree.

"O Lord, protect him. He's a-fixin' to get himself killed," mama said stifling a scream.

"Get killed nothing," Gussie hissed. "He's fixing to kill somebody else." She darted down the stairs and out the back door, and just as daddy raised his long pistol and pointed it at the back of the man's head, Gussie darted through the trees and grabbed his arms. The two of them fell to the ground just as the man struck a match to light a cherry bomb.

"Dadgum it, Gussie," daddy yelled. "Turn me loose. I had a bead right on his ear."

The man with the match whirled and looked. Just as he did Sam cut loose with his sixteen-gauge shotgun. He had drawn a bead too, but it wasn't on the man's ear—it was on the seat of his pants.

There was a howl of pain as the shadowy figure grabbed his backside and danced out of the trees. Sam fired the other barrel as the man took off down the gravel road, kicking his heels high in the air.

Gussie dragged daddy, still kicking and shouting, back into the house. But the fight was over. The mob disappeared into the night, and we never had any more trouble as long as we lived in Ford City.

Chapter Ten

Just suppose God searched through Heaven,
He couldn't find one willing to be
The supreme sacrifice that was needed,
That would buy eternal life for you and me.

Oh! Had it not been for a place called Mount Calv'ry,
Had it not been for the old rugged cross;
Had it not been for a Man called Jesus,
Then forever my soul would be lost.
                    —RUSTY GOODMAN

Rusty was always the rebel in the Goodman family. Not that my sisters didn't do their share of rebelling, but Rusty just seemed to have a rebel streak in him. The rest of us had been content to sit under the brush arbor and listen to the singing, preaching, and shouting. But Rusty was the one who was always restless and fidgety in the meetings.

One night, back in the old brush arbor at the Twilly Town Church of God near Dora, Rusty sneaked out of the service and went around behind the pavilion. There he found four or five of the "big" boys standing in the shadows smoking "roll-your-own" cigarettes. Rusty was about six years old and was fascinated as the boys blew smoke from their noses. Suddenly he was aware of a big figure directly behind him. Before he had a chance to turn he felt daddy's strong fingers grab his ear. His feet barely touched the ground as he was pulled back into the circle of light. They marched directly down the aisle to the front

149

row. Daddy's face was stern, and Rusty skipped along painfully behind, trying to keep daddy from pulling his ear off.

Daddy plopped Rusty down hard on the front bench and gave his ear an extra twist just to let him know he meant business. Then daddy marched back down the aisle to his place in the shadows. Rusty sat there in his little bib overalls, hanging his head. Rusty's face was red with embarrassment and his ear stung with pain. I sensed then that there were wild thoughts of rebellion racing through his mind. I was right, and when he became fourteen these thoughts began to take form.

Rusty had an exceptionally keen mind. Even though we often moved several times in one school year, he always seemed to be able to catch up. When we arrived in Ford City, he was promoted into Colbert County Junior High School and made good grades.

But Rusty's love was music. Several years earlier daddy had bought him an old guitar. Rusty had strung some wires on it, patched a big hole in the back, glued a new bridge in place, and learned to play it by himself. Sometimes he would sit on the back porch all afternoon playing three chords—open G, C, and D. He was about to drive the rest of us crazy.

We hadn't been in Ford City long when I had a chance to preach in Jackson, Tennessee. The entire family went along (as usual), and when the series of meetings was over, I took Rusty into a music store and made a down payment on an ebony-black, six-stringed, Gibson steel guitar. I'd never seen a boy so happy over anything in all my life. The unit also contained a little split suitcase amplifier and loudspeaker that we could hook up to a small, bullet-shaped microphone. So, not only did Rusty get his steel guitar, but the Goodman family purchased their first sound system.

Almost overnight Rusty became an expert on the steel guitar. Little Roy Wiggins was his idol along with Jerry Byrd. He had heard both on the radio, and it wasn't long before he had perfectly copied Jerry Byrd's style. At the age of fourteen he was recognized as one of the smoothest guitar players in Alabama.

It wasn't long before he was receiving offers from local bands and combos. The rebel blood began to surge in his veins.

The first explosion came at school. Rusty often missed as much as three days a week because he was out singing with the family. One morning the math teacher shook her finger in his face and said, "Charles, either you start coming to school like the other children, or I'll have to take you to the principal." Rusty's rebel blood boiled and he sassed her back saying, "It ain't no skin off your nose if I don't come to school."

The teacher turned on her heel and started down the hall toward the principal's office. Rusty started in the opposite direction, out the door and all the way home. It was his last day at school.

Sam had already dropped out of school, and Rusty's steel guitar was a welcome addition to our street meetings on a regular basis. These street meetings were usually Saturday afternoon affairs in the towns within driving distance of Ford City. We would pick a town that was having an auction, and after singing for awhile, we passed the hat. Then we'd pile in our old car and "hit" three or four other nearby towns before dark.

Our method was simple. We had a big, car-top loudspeaker that was strapped on our little red car. Sam was our "field man" and would scout around and find a store or barber shop near our street-corner location. Taking our long, black extension cord he would brazenly walk into the shop and ask to "borrow some juice." We would then begin our service.

Experience taught us to take the offering before I preached. The folks loved to stand and listen to the music, but when I started preaching and stepping on toes, the old farmers would often spit their tobacco on the street and wander back to the auction. The one thing I did insist on was giving an altar call at the close of each service. We were singing to make a living, but I was preaching because God had called me to preach. Without fail people would step forward from the crowd and kneel with me on the sidewalk.

Usually Rusty would play an invitation hymn during the altar call. I had made a couple of suggestions concerning appropriate hymns but Rusty was a rebel. I discovered this one afternoon when we were holding a street service in a little one-horse town near the Mississippi border. After I finished preaching, I said, "Now I want you good folks to bow your heads in prayer while my little brother plays a song during the altar call."

The people had been moved by the sermon and several were on the verge of tears. I felt if Rusty would play a sweet, sentimental hymn the folks would respond. I stepped back and looked at Rusty. He was all set, but I was concerned about the devilish glint in his eye. I had reason to be concerned, for the first notes of the "invitation" hymn made me shudder. He was playing a jazzed-up version of the "Steel Guitar Rag." The volume was turned up all the way and his bare foot, propped against the fender of the car, was stomping in wicked time to the music. Sam suddenly got the spirit and joined in on the rhythm guitar. I sighed, shook my head and looked out at the crowd of people who moments before had been standing reverently with bowed heads. They were grinning, patting their feet, and some were even clapping in time with the music. I daresay it was the strangest invitation hymn ever played in the history of street preaching.

In July of that year we met J. I. Nunn in Moulton, Alabama. Word had gotten out that the Goodmans had a sound system. Any singing group that could afford a sound system was always invited to the big singings—whether they were any good or not —so the other groups could use their equipment.

J. I. Nunn ran a little jewelry store in Moulton. A bespectacled, graying man, he also promoted the First Sunday Singings in the upstairs of the Lawrence County Court House in Moulton. On that first Sunday afternoon the people were packed into that little upstairs room. It was hot and the hand fans, furnished by the local funeral parlor, were waving back and forth. The thermometer that hung on an old oak tree outside the court house registered 100 degrees, but it must have been at least 130 in that crowded upstairs room. All seven of the Goodmans were crowded around our little bullet mike. We had the vocal sound turned up as loud as we could but Rusty's steel guitar was even louder.

During the intermission Rusty overheard Mr. Nunn talking to his wife. "Them Goodmans are good singers, all right. Only they'd be a heap better off if they'd leave that hillbilly guitar at home."

Rusty's heart was broken. He had dreams of becoming a famous guitarist. He never realized there were some people, like Brother Nunn, that thought it highly improper to combine gospel music with the sounds of a guitar.

That evening Rusty and I had a long talk. "Howard," Rusty said as we sat on the front steps of the house, "I'm just not cut out for this kind of music. You and Sam feel the Lord is calling you to do this. But I'm just a misfit. You all ain't ashamed of the gospel. You don't ever back down on nothing. You've got this burden for souls. You love to pray with folks and talk to them about the Lord. But me, I'm different. I'm ashamed of having to go out in public barefooted with my pants rolled up. I want to make something of myself. I want to be a big name in music. Folks have been telling me I could make the Grand Old Opry right now if I'd just practice a little more. I've been listening to Eddy Arnold over the radio and I'm learning to sing his songs. Every night I dream of standing on the stage in the Opry, singing Eddy Arnold songs and accompanying myself on the steel guitar. I know I can make it, Howard, and I want out of the family group to try."

I sensed there was something deeper bothering Rusty than just his dreams and ambitions. "Did what Mr. Nunn said this afternoon make you feel this way?"

Rusty dropped his head. "I guess so. But maybe he's right. Maybe we shouldn't mix gospel music with guitar music. Some folks think that guitars are of the devil."

"Do you feel that way, Rusty?" I asked.

He looked up at me, his eyes wide with determination. "No, sir," he answered, "I feel the Lord can be honored as much with a guitar as he can with a pipe organ."

"Then why all this talk about running away and joining the Opry just because someone criticized your playing? Listen to your critics, Rusty. Don't run from them. You can always learn. Maybe your volume was too high. But that's no reason to quit and run away."

We were sitting on the front steps of the old Sherman house, and it was almost dark. Rusty was staring at the tops of the big old cedar trees, lost in thought. I continued, "Rusty, lots of folks don't like my preaching. That's what almost got us killed right here in Ford City. But I ain't gonna quit just because some folks throw rocks and firecrackers at me. They whipped our Lord. The people got so mad they crucified Him. Now if Jesus didn't back down, then neither will I—even if they kill me."

Rusty was still staring at the treetops. The last rays of sunset had disappeared from the sky and only the sound of the whip-poorwill was heard from a nearby bush. "I guess you think I'm some kind of a quitter, don't you?"

I reached over and put my arm around his shoulder. "No, sir, I don't think you're a quitter. I think you're a real fighter. But you don't fight by running away. You fight by holding your ground and claiming the promise of Jesus that He will never leave us nor forsake us."

Rusty slowly nodded his head. Standing up he walked down the old wooden steps and stood in the dirt path. He was still deep in thought. "I think I'll take a walk for awhile. I've got a lot of things to think about."

"That's good," I replied. "I'll just wait right here and pray for you while you think." And I did.

The next Saturday afternoon we were in a little town called Cloverdale, up near the Tennessee border. They were having a county fair and a lot of people were in town. We had a good singing service and took up an offering that amounted to almost twenty dollars. I had preached and then cautiously asked Rusty to play a song on his steel guitar while I gave the altar call.

I stepped back and closed my eyes. Suddenly the soft, haunting strains of an old gospel song, "Down on Your Knees," came floating from the speakers. I had been trying to get Rusty to learn that song for months, but he was more interested in the "Steel Guitar Rag." The beautiful melody faded away. I stepped forward and with choked voice gave the altar call. I wiped my eyes and when I looked out there was Rusty, kneeling on that old hard curbstone, his face turned to heaven and his cheeks bathed in tears—giving his heart to the Lord.

I don't know whether anyone else answered the invitation that afternoon or not. All I know is that there was great rejoicing in heaven—and in the Goodman family circle—as my little brother came to Jesus.

Chapter Eleven

I've been trav'ling here in this life,
With its heartache, trouble and strife,
Sometimes Satan tries to tell me to turn aside;
I say "Satan get thee behind, No returning in me you'll find,
I'm too near my heavenly home where I'll abide.

I'm too near to home with my Lord,
Too near home and heaven's reward,
I'm not returning to sin, I have made my vow;
There's nothing to go back to,
Oh Praise God sweet heaven's in view,
I'm too near my heavenly home to turn back now.

—CHARLES WYCUFF

The problem of whether the Goodmans were going to keep
a guitar to accompany their gospel singing was soon settled. We
couldn't make the payments and had to send it back. However,
we were certain of one thing: gospel music and guitars definitely
go together. It was this conviction that would eventually lead
the Goodmans to the top.

There was another factor that was to play a tremendous role
in sending the Goodmans to the front ranks of gospel music.
That was the addition of a young soprano to the group.

It began with our introduction to Cat Freeman, a tenor from
Sand Mountain, Alabama. Several years had passed and I had
gone to work with Reverend C. T. Douglas. He was preaching

156

and I was singing, and we were broadcasting over WSGN in Birmingham. When we heard Cat Freeman was in town, we asked him to join our group.

Brother Douglas lined up a tent revival meeting on Sand Mountain near Albertville. Cat went with us and on opening night he introduced us to his family. I shook hands with his mother and father, but the one who caught and held my attention was his pretty sixteen-year-old sister. She was a beauty queen in the local high school and just about the prettiest thing I'd ever seen. Her name was Vestel.

That night, on the way back to Birmingham, I told Brother Douglas, "I met my wife tonight."

"Aw, Brother Howard," he drawled, "you don't mean it. You're just joking. That girl's just sixteen and you're twenty-five."

"No, I do mean it."

"Well," Brother Douglas grinned, "you're sure gonna have one hard time courting her 'cause Cat won't let her date gospel singers."

"What?" I almost shouted, sitting up straight in the seat. "How come?"

"You ain't been around too many gospel singers, Howard," he said. "Most of 'em are mostly 'singer' and not much 'gospel.' You think they're all like you and Sam—dedicated to the Lord. But that ain't the way it is. Cat knows better too. He's been around gospel singers most of his life and he knows what most of them are like. He's not about to turn that pretty little sister of his loose with some hot-lipped gadabout. I don't know how he feels about you, but I do know that he's told me several times he'd kill the first gospel singer that tried to date Vestel."

"O my soul," I moaned, slumping down in the seat beside Brother Douglas. "I find my wife and right away somebody's trying to kill me. It's the story of my life."

It took me almost four years before I was ready to marry Vestel—during which time we never had a single date. I wrote her letters off and on, but our family was constantly on the

move and I just didn't have time to get serious. We moved to
Kimberly, then back to Birmingham, and finally to Lanett
where I was pastor of a church for a year. Later we moved to
LaGrange and finally to the little town of Wingo, Kentucky,
just outside of Mayfield where we were given time on the radio
to sing and promote our meetings.

I had been writing to Vestel occasionally during this time,
but seldom saw her. In the fall of 1949 we went to Gadsden,
Alabama, for a Sunday night singing. I planned to drive back
to Huntsville for a meeting Tuesday night. While I was in the
vicinity I stopped by to see an old friend, a man who also knew
Vestel—Brother Bonds.

"I'm gonna tell you something, Brother Howard," he said.
"If you want that Vestel Freeman, you better go after her."

"What do you mean, Brother Bonds? I've been writing to her
occasionally and she never has said anything was wrong."

Brother Bonds looked up at me from where he was sitting in
an old, cane-bottom chair near the wood stove. "Now let me
tell you a thing or two about women, Brother Howard. You've
been writing Vestel Freeman once every six months. That's not
enough if you have hopes of getting married. She falls in love
with some local boy and decides to get married, and then along
comes one of your sweet love letters and it tears her all to pieces.
You just can't treat a woman like that. A woman needs to be
loved—all the time. Not just twice a year on paper."

I started to interrupt but he continued on. "Vestel's in love
with you and you've been treating her like a dog. She's been
going with a boy named Jerome and has finally consented to
marry him. Yet when she heard over the radio that you were
singing in Gadsden and Huntsville, she borrowed her daddy's
car and came flying over here Sunday afternoon thinking you'd
stop by. She told me to tell you that if you went back to Kentucky this time without seeing her that you needn't ever write
again. Now here it is Tuesday and I imagine she's about given
up on you. You may be too late already."

"What do you mean, too late already?" I asked.

"She's already had her blood tests and is gonna marry this other guy. If you want her, you sure better go after her."

I didn't waste any time. After leaving Brother Bonds I drove directly to Albertville and out to the Freeman farm. Pulling up in the yard I saw Vestel at the clothesline, dressed in faded bluejeans with her shirttail hanging out.

"Howard Goodman!" she screamed, running for the house. "That's just like you. I wait around here for a year and then you come pulling up without giving me any warning."

Moments later, though, she was out of the house and greeting me warmly.

We sat in my old car and talked. "I'm going to Huntsville for a concert tonight," I said. "I can't stay long now but I'll be back over on Thursday."

She looked me straight in the eye. "I guess you know I'm engaged to another boy, don't you?"

"Yes. Brother Bonds told me all about it."

"Jerome's in Detroit earning enough money to rent us an apartment. As soon as he's ready, he's coming for me. He could be back tonight or not until Christmas. I don't know." She paused and looked out of the car window at a couple of old white chickens scratching in the side yard. "I love you, Howard. I'll wait until Thursday. But if you let me down this time it will be the last."

I was back Thursday. Vestel's church held a Thursday night prayer meeting and I arrived just after they started. Walking in the front door, I came straight down the aisle and took a seat beside Vestel. The fact that she was engaged to the son of one of the church leaders was well known. My arrival caused a great stir among the congregation. There was a rustle of whispers accompanied by hushed "ooohhhs" and "aaahhhs" as Vestel looked up at me, smiled, and scooted over on the bench so I could sit down.

Ignoring the craning necks of the old ladies who were looking to see who the strange man was, I turned and said in a loud whisper, "Can you go to Nashville with me for the singing? I'll bring you back."

The two old ladies sitting directly behind us who were leaning forward to catch every word gulped and gasped. One of them let out a shocked "Aaahhh!" which could be heard all over the little church.

Vestel seemed to be enjoying the excitement. "I don't know. When are you going?"

Shocked beyond imagination that Vestel Freeman would even listen to such an outrageous offer, much less consider it, the man and woman sitting in front of us turned completely around and gave Vestel a hard stare.

By now it seemed that every ear in the little church was tuned in on our conversation. I replied, "We're going tonight. We gotta get to Nashville early in the morning."

Suddenly realizing that even the preacher had stopped talking and was straining to hear our conversation, I lowered my voice and continued. "Ruth and Stella are in Nashville and you can stay with them. Just go ask your mother if you can go."

"She won't hear to it," Vestel objected. "Not with you. I'm engaged to Jerome. That's his folks sitting right over there." She motioned with her eyes while her head remained motionless. I glanced to where she indicated and my eyes collided with the coldest, sternest look I'd ever received from anyone.

Vestel finally got up and walked down the aisle to where her mother was sitting on the front row. She sat down beside her, but her mother continued looking straight ahead, totally ignoring Vestel's presence. "Mom, I'm going to Nashville with Howard tonight."

"You're what?" she shouted, turning and looking at Vestel like she'd lost her mind. I could feel the holes being bored in the back of my neck by a hundred fierce eyes from all over the congregation. I felt like some evil seducer who had slithered into the congregation of the righteous. I could almost smell the tar and feathers being prepared in the name of the Lord.

"Mom," Vestel continued, "Cat's in Nashville. He's singing with the Statesmen Quartet. As soon as I get there, I'll go stay with him."

Mrs. Freeman could see that her nineteen-year-old daughter

had her mind already made up. "Well, you go talk to your daddy. If he says it's all right, we'll talk about it when I get home."

"No, mom, we've got to go right now. Howard wants to leave right away."

Mrs. Freeman turned slowly and stared back at me. Every head in the church turned with her. I just sat there, grinning and nodding my head at all my new fans.

Mrs. Freeman shook her head in resignation. "He looks harmless. You go check with your daddy. Whatever he says will be all right."

Vestel jumped up from her seat and almost ran back down the aisle to my seat. "Mom says O.K. All I gotta do is ask daddy."

Another "ooohhh" of shock went up from the congregation. Obviously they didn't share Mrs. Freeman's feeling that I was harmless. I quickly got to my feet and whispered, "I got a feeling we better get out of here."

Vestel glanced at the hostile faces and nodded. "You're right." We headed for the rear of the church.

Just as we reached the double doors that led to the porch, they swung open. A small, dark-headed young man walked in. We stood momentarily face to face as he stared first at Vestel then at me. Vestel turned white as a sheet and looked at the floor. Grabbing my arm she pulled me through the door and out into the churchyard where my car was parked. By this time she was running, dragging me behind her. Confused, I turned and looked back over my shoulder. The young man had stepped back out onto the porch and was watching us. His hands were on his hips and his mouth open in shock and amazement.

"Let's get out of here," Vestel whispered as she tugged me along. "Quick, get the car started."

Thoroughly confused, I jumped in the car while she clambered in from the other side, rolling up the window and locking the door. Moments later we were whirling out of the parking lot. Vestel cast one more look out the rear window at the young man who had now run out in the parking lot and was vainly trying to motion us back.

"Who in the world was that?" I finally blurted out. "He scared you to death."

Vestel slipped down in the seat and put her hands over her face. "That was Jerome. He said as soon as he saved enough money he was coming home to marry me. Now here he is."

We drove directly to Vestel's house where she called her daddy. The old-fashioned crank phone hung on the wall, and Vestel gave the crank a vigorous whirl and cast nervous glances at the door as if she expected Jerome to burst in any moment.

Mr. Freeman, a quiet, dignified man, ran a little barber shop in Fyffe, a few miles from Albertville. He had to work late at night and was just closing the shop when the phone rang.

"Daddy," Vestel said breathlessly, "I'm going to Nashville with Howard. We're going down to Gadsden and spend the night with the Dixons first. But when we get to Nashville, I'll stay with Cat."

Vestel and I were both bending over the telephone, our heads glued together and the earphone jammed in between. I could barely hear Mr. Freeman's voice.

"Well, I don't know, baby. You just do whatever you feel like's right."

"Thank you, daddy. I knew you'd understand."

"It's not gonna look good, you know."

"I'll take the consequences."

"Jerome's gonna have a fit. He came by the barber shop to ask where you was and I told him you was at church."

"I know," Vestel said, glancing nervously at the door, "I saw him there."

"Well, just be careful—and be good," Mr. Freeman said.

Vestel hung up and shouted, "It'll take me two minutes to get my stuff. You get the car started." Moments later we were on our way—long before mama, Mr. Freeman, or Jerome could arrive to disrupt our plans.

Friday night we were in Nashville at Ryman Auditorium, the home of the Grand Old Opry. Wally Fowler promoted a big all-night singing on the first Friday of each month. Just before ·the show started I walked up to Mr. Fowler and said, "Say, Wally, I got my future wife with me tonight. We're gonna get married."

Wally said, "Aw, Howard, you're crazy. You ain't gonna get married. You've hardly ever been out with a girl. Who'd have you?"

"You just wait here and I'll show you."

Moments later I was back with Vestel, introducing her to Wally. He looked her over and gave a low whistle. "So, you're Cat Freeman's sister. Well I'll say this much for Howard, he may have waited a long time but he sure picked a winner."

Vestel glanced up at me, her pretty forehead wrinkled in puzzlement. "What's he mean, you've waited a long time? Waited for what?"

Wally broke out laughing. "Why Howard just announced that you was his future wife."

"Howard Goodman," Vestel half screamed. "You haven't said a word to me about marriage. Now you've gone and announced it to all Nashville."

Wally was up to the occasion. Putting his arms around both of us he said, "Tell you what. Let's do it next month. You all can be married right here on the stage of the Grand Old Opry. It'll be the first Friday in December and everybody will have the Christmas spirit. We'll broadcast the ceremony and my sponsors will donate entire rooms of furniture. You all will not only be famous, but you'll be rich too when we finish. It should be the biggest thing to hit Nashville in years."

"Great," I exclaimed. "It sounds wonderful. What about it, honey?"

Vestel was too shaken by the sudden turn of events to choke out a comment. She just stood there, grinning and nodding her head.

After the show we drove all night, arriving in Haleyville, Alabama, at 6:00 A.M. Saturday morning. Ruth and Vestel got a room in the old hotel and went directly to bed. At 10:00 A.M. I knocked on the door. Vestel's sleepy voice came from the other side. "Who's there?"

"It's me, Howard. I better go call your daddy and tell him

that we can't get home today. We've got to sing over in Fulton, Mississippi, tonight and then be at a church between here and Jasper on Sunday afternoon. I'm gonna tell him I'll get you home Monday."

Vestel was wide awake now, hurrying to the door. "Wait just a minute until I get my robe on," she said excitedly. Opening the door she peered out. "Whatever you do, don't call mama. Call daddy. You can talk him into it, but if you call mama, she'll skin you alive."

I kissed her forehead and dashed down the stairs to the lobby where I placed a long-distance call to Freeman's Barber Shop in Fyffe. The phone rang three times before Mr. Freeman answered.

"Eeehhh? Huhhh?" he said, straining to hear me as I shouted into the phone.

"This is Howard," I bellowed.

"Yeaaa. Where are you?" I could tell he was shouting into his ancient phone too.

"We're in Haleyville.

"Yeaaa! What are you doing in Haleyville?"

"I got your daughter over here."

"Yeaaa! I know that."

"I just can't possibly get her home till Monday."

"You said you'd get her home today."

"I know, but we've got to sing in Mississippi tonight. Now there's nothing to worry about. My sisters are here and she's with them. There's no harm that can come to her."

"Well, all right then. You all be careful."

"I will. You don't worry about her one bit."

"Okay. I won't."

I heard the phone click down on the other end, and I walked across the lobby and stood standing in the door of the hotel that led out onto the street. "Thank you, Lord," I breathed. "I don't know what you're fixing to do, but whatever it is, I got a feeling I'm sure gonna like it."

That night, Saturday, the Goodmans sang in concert in the high school in Fulton. The next afternoon we appeared in a little church out in the hills between Jasper and Haleyville for an all-day singing with eatin' on the ground.

It was chilly and the wind whistled through the cracks in the walls of the old clapboard building. The little church was nestled in a grove of poplar trees that stretched naked limbs toward the cold, gray sky. But the people were warm and friendly, and we arrived just in time for dinner on the ground. Long planks were balanced on wooden sawhorses situated between the old graveyard and the little white church. They had been covered with newspapers and groaned under the weight of the "covered dishes" brought in from the surrounding hills in old cars and mule-drawn wagons. Baked ham, meat loaf, meat balls and gravy, baked yams, boiled turnips, sausage and grits, hot biscuits, macaroni "pie," field peas and fatback, banana pudding, and the biggest assortment of pies and cakes I'd ever seen. It was the kind of meeting that brought joy to the hearts and stomachs of Goodmans.

After filling our plates, Vestel and I sat on the ground and talked and ate. When we finished, I helped her to her feet and we walked over to our car sitting in the parking lot. Slipping into the front seat we closed the door to keep warm. For a long time we sat looking at the crowds of country people.

Turning to Vestel, I placed my hand on top of hers and said, "Let's forget about Wally Fowler's offer and get married right away. If I take you back home without marrying you, there's gonna be a lot of gossip. I don't care if the girls have been with us, you know what it will be like around Sand Mountain. To save all that talk, why don't we go ahead and tie the knot?"

Vestel looked at me, her pretty face clouded with the difficulty of making a decision. "But I'm engaged."

"I ain't worried none about that," I said bravely. "Are you?"

A tiny smile played around the corners of her mouth as she said, "No."

"Then will you marry me tomorrow?"

"Yes," she said. Reaching over she put her arms gently around my neck and tenderly placed her lips against mine. "Oh yes," she murmured.

We almost forgot we were supposed to sing that afternoon. Stella finally rapped on the window of the car and shouted, "You two can hold hands and stare at each other later. The folks are waiting for us inside."

We got out of the car and headed for the church building. I had Vestel by the hand as I announced to Stella, "We've decided to get married tomorrow."

Stella let out a whoop and reached over and hugged Vestel's neck. As we took our place on the stage, Stella walked to the microphone and said, "I have an announcement I'd like to make. I want to introduce our future sister-in-law Vestel Freeman."

The roar of applause shook the rafters. I guess most of the folks suspected that something was up, the way Vestel and I had been acting in the car. I couldn't tell whether the applause was in joy or relief. Whatever, it sure made me feel good inside.

We were married Monday in Fulton, and Tuesday morning we headed home.

"I'm scared to face mama," Vestel whimpered as we neared Sand Mountain. "She's always dreamed of a big church wedding for me. I don't know what she'll say now."

"Well, I've prayed about it," I said confidently, "and I know the Lord will take care of things."

"He sure better," Vestel said, her voice tight, " 'cause mama sure has one whale of a temper when she gets mad."

Mama Freeman was in the yard in front of the little frame farmhouse. She had an old broom in her hand, vigorously sweeping the loose dirt and leaves out of the hard, packed-dirt yard.

She stopped and put her hands on her hips as we drove up. "Well, if this ain't a pretty sight," she said.

Vestel sat in the car while I got out to make some kind of explanation.

"There ain't no use telling me what you've done," she said.
"I know."

"You think you know?" I asked.

"Yes, I sure do."

"Well, in case you're doubting it, we went and got married last night."

"I knowed it," Mama Freeman screamed throwing her broom to the ground and grinning. "Come here, child," she cried out to Vestel who was cowering in the seat of the car. "Come here and let your mama hug you."

Vestel jumped out and ran to her mother's open arms. Mrs. Freeman turned to me. "And you too, Howard. I'd hug you but I can't get my arms around you so I'll just have to kiss your face."

Jerome heard we were back in town and that night he drove out to the farm. He was drunk and had already wrecked his car three times that day. All he did was roar around and around in front of the house, his tires throwing loose gravel and spinning in the dirt. He was blowing his horn, shouting, and cursing. We stayed inside and let him work out his anger. Going out to talk to him just didn't seem to be a wise thing to do.

Jerome soon married another local girl and returned to Detroit where he opened a tavern. God's planning and timing were becoming more and more evident. I don't think Vestel would have made a good wife for a bartender, and I know that the addition of her sweet, soft soprano voice to the Goodman sound was one of the things that began to move us up the ladder to success.

Chapter Twelve

I want to see Jesus; look upon His face;
Meet all the people who have gone there by His grace;
Hear the angel choir sing songs of Zion and make them ring,
But most of all I want to see Jesus more than anything.

—BOBBY GOODMAN

Vestel and I moved into the back bedroom of the big house in Wingo, Kentucky, just south of Mayfield. She had often sung with her own family so she fit right in with the Goodmans. We had a daily radio program at noon on WNGO, and as our popularity grew, we received more and more invitations to sing in neighboring cities. Gussie had rejoined us, so the whole family was singing, with even little Bobby joining on some occasions.

Our financial situation was improving. The offerings at singings were improving too, sometimes running as high as one hundred fifty dollars. Of course, there were always the exceptions. Typical of the exceptions was Russellville, Alabama. We had been to Winfield for a fifth-Sunday, all-day singing and were dead tired. At the close of the service a promoter came up and said, "I sponsor a regular fifth-Sunday-night singing convention in a big church in Russellville. You folks have to go right through there on your way back home. I'd sure love to have you stop by and sing for us."

I looked around at the rest of the family. We were dead tired but we needed the money. The promoter, seeing we were having difficulty deciding, said, "Of course, they'll take up an offering. If you folks stop by, we'll treat you right."

"We're mighty tired and hungry," I said, "but maybe we'll come on just the same and make a full day out of it."

"Hungry, are you?" the promoter said. "Let me tell you what I'll do. My sister owns a restaurant in Russellville. You just name whatever you want and it'll be ready for you when you get there."

Now that sounded great. At least we'd get a dinner out of the deal. We all ordered fried chicken and started packing our things in order to get there on time.

The promoter's sister did have a nice restaurant, and we ate our fill of chicken. After we finished we went around to the church for the concert. They had a packed house and we sang for two straight hours. Even though we were tired, we felt like we had done a good job.

Just before they dismissed, the promoter got up and said, "Folks, we've got a few incidental expenses and we want you to help us with them."

Sam poked me in the ribs. "Oh-oh, we're in trouble. I guess we're one of the incidentals."

But the worst was yet to come. "Now we're not asking anybody to sacrifice. A nickel or a dime will be fine. Don't feel obligated, just give what you can."

I heard Sam moan and slump down in his seat.

They passed the offering plate and after the meeting the promoter came up to me and said, "Well, we took up eight dollars and thirty-four cents for you all."

I felt we were lucky. At least that would buy us gas back home. The man started counting out the money. When he finished, he said, "Now let's see, we let you have those chicken dinners at a discount so they only came to five dollars and thirty cents. That's not bad for all them good chicken dinners is it?" he said as he pocketed the five dollars and thirty cents and handed me the balance—three dollars and four cents.

I just stood there, holding the loose change in my hand. He slapped me on the back. "Yes, sir, we always enjoy the Goodmans. You all be sure and come back the next time we have a big singing like this."

I didn't have the heart to tell the rest of the family until after

we had started the long ride back home. I thought they were
going to tear the roof out of the car when I broke the news. A
couple of the girls wanted to turn around and go back. I don't
know what they had in mind, but I felt the best thing to do was
put as many miles between us and Russellville as I could.

"I'll tell you one thing," Sam grumbled as he slumped down in
the seat of the car while we rolled through the night, "it'll be a
long time before I eat any more fried chicken."

Weekends were spent on the street corners. Many of the
mining companies paid their workers every two weeks. On Saturday afternoon there would be as many as five hundred men
waiting at the payroll office. They would go into town in the
morning and let their wives shop while they stood in line at the
payroll office waiting for the Brink's truck to unload their money.
We would gather on the corner and sing for them until they got
their pay. After they picked up their envelopes they would come
by and give us an offering—sometimes as high as two hundred
dollars. We were grateful, too, because without their support the
Goodman family would never have made it.

Occasionally we ran into opposition over the love offerings. A
promoter, Jess Dixon, had invited us to sing at a first-Sunday
singing in Newbern, Tennessee. Jess got up and said, "I asked
these people over from Wingo this afternoon. I want you to give
them a good freewill offering."

An old man, sitting about three rows from the front, jumped to
his feet. "Well, I'll tell you the way I feel about it. We've got too
many good singers in this county that need our money. I'm agin'
giving it to a bunch of folks from out-of-state."

An uncomfortable hush fell over the packed auditorium as the
man sat down. Jess Dixon, flustered and a little angry, stepped
back to the microphone. "Well, I feel obligated because these are
the finest singers and the best bunch of folks in the country. You
don't have to give anything if you don't want, but I'm going
to give them twenty dollars for their gas."

Another man stood up and said, "Wait a minute. That old

skinflint over there may not want to give anything, but I do. Here's ten dollars to help out, too."

Another man jumped to his feet waving a five dollar bill. "If someone will come back here and get this, I'll add it to the kitty." Others stood to their feet or raised their hands and in less than five minutes they had collected more than one hundred dollars. A thirty-dollar love offering would have been all we would have received had they passed the plates. We left praising the Lord for cantankerous people.

After living in Wingo for two years, we moved to Evansville, Indiana, and made a down payment on a big, ten-room, frame house in the run-down section of Evansville. The entire family moved in, including some in-laws, nieces, and nephews. Vestel and I had taken Gussie's daughter, LaBreeska, to raise. It seemed the family was growing larger by the day while the income was growing smaller.

We did manage to get on several radio stations, including stations in Evansville, Booneville, and Mt. Carmel. All were live, daily programs either fifteen or thirty minutes long. Every day we piled in the car and made the circuit, going from one town to another to broadcast. We always closed by saying, "If you want the Goodman family to sing for you, you can contact us in care of this station."

But in time our group began to break up and the invitations were less frequent. Sam had been drafted. Vestel was pregnant and unable to travel much of the time. And on top of this, Rusty's rebellious nature was getting harder and harder to live with. We were going in the hole financially, and I knew things would have to break before long.

Rusty had acquired a great deal of musical knowledge and was playing the guitar like an expert. His idol was Perry Como, whose singing style Rusty had nearly perfected. But his big problem was that he was full of advice—which he never failed to give.

"Howard," Rusty said one time, "you can't sing that song like that."

"What do you mean, we can't sing it like that? We've been singing it like that for years."

"Then you've been singing it wrong. I've been studying the music and that particular song calls for a chord progression from C to D^7 to G^7 and then back to C. You've been skipping the D^7 and jumping to G^7."

Being older than Rusty, I was irritated by his suggestions (even though I knew the Lord had given him a good ear for music). "Rusty, you may be right, but as long as I'm leading this group you'll sing it like I tell you. I've never had a music lesson in my life and I don't know anything about D^7s and G^7s. I just know how I want it to sound and that's that."

Rusty was mad. He knew he was right, and it frustrated him that I wouldn't listen. "Well, I don't have to stay with this outfit," he stormed. "Hovie Lister told me I had the best voice in the business, and I can go with any male quartet I want. If I wasn't about to be drafted, I'd leave right now."

He turned and stomped out of the room, calling back over his shoulder, "And I'll tell you something else. Don't look for me back when I get out of the army. If Elvis Presley can make it big, so can I."

Rusty was drafted the following month, and three weeks later Ricky was born. Even though we were thanking the Lord for the baby's safe arrival, things were beginning to look dark as the Goodman family began to break up.

After a time we left Evansville and moved to Augusta, Georgia. Prospects were bleak there and just when we decided we'd made another mistake, Jack Thomas, the manager of the radio station in Swainsboro, Georgia, called us.

"I'm building a big auditorium down here for gospel singing," he said. "If you all will move down, I'll give you time on the station and a percentage of the gate at the singings." We traded our old DeSoto for a 1952 Chrysler and arrived in Swainsboro in style.

Mr. Thomas's Quonset-hut type auditorium seated twenty-two hundred people and a big singing was held once a month. Radio contracts came pouring in, and once again we were busy with weekend singings. We stayed in Swainsboro two years during which time Vicki was born. However, at the end of the period, problems began to develop with Mr. Thomas. He had guaranteed us a certain percentage of the gross intake. However, as our popularity spread and the income increased, he began to welsh on his part of the bargain.

"If I pay you what I agreed to pay you," he argued, "you folks would be making more than me. Now that don't seem right, do it?"

"Well, it don't seem right for you to promise us something and then not pay it, either," I replied.

By the end of 1955 we saw it was a hopeless cause. When an offer came from WLOS-TV in Asheville, North Carolina, we packed up our belongings and left for the mountains.

We never dreamed we would ever be on TV. Channel 13 had a wide viewing audience throughout the Blue Ridge Mountains of North Carolina and could be received as far south as Greenwood, South Carolina. It seemed like we'd finally gotten the big break we'd prayed for.

Through our daily, live TV program on Channel 13, we got hooked up with a hillbilly called Cousin Milburn who had a popular country music show on the same station. "Cous" had a tremendous following back in the mountains. He was promoting a big July 4 celebration on his farm outside of Asheville and asked us to help him, agreeing to give us 25 percent of the gate. We helped clean off the farm, built a stage, and marked off a parking lot. The big Independence Day celebration included gospel, hillbilly, country, and western singing as well as fireworks and a stage show. He charged fifty cents a head and sold concessions once the folks got inside.

Twenty thousand people showed up that afternoon. It was one of the biggest shows ever produced in the mountains of western North Carolina. The day after the program Cousin Milburn came around and gave me six hundred dollars.

"Cous, you announced on your TV show that we had twenty thousand folks present yesterday."

"That's right," he said grinning, "it was about the biggest thing we've ever had around here, wasn't it?"

"Well, at fifty cents a head, that amounts to ten thousand dollars you took in. You promised us 25 percent of the gate which means you should have given us twenty-five hundred dollars rather than six hundred."

"I'm sorry about that, Howard," he said, "but I had some incidental expenses to take care of. That's the best I can do."

"Cous," I said firmly, "where we come from a man's word is his bond. If you went in the hole, we'll be glad to help you out. But I don't believe you did. I think you made money, big money. And I don't think it's right to take advantage of us this way."

Cous's entire attitude changed. He smiled arrogantly and said, "Well, that's your tough luck, fella. You should have signed a contract. Over here we do things differently and if you ignorant, backwoods folks can't keep up, then you oughta shove off."

The next day Cous made fun of us on his daily TV program. "There's some stupid gospel singers around here (I won't call their names) but they got a group of fat girls singing with them, and if you ain't careful they'll try to fleece you good."

We were broken-hearted. Being beaten out of our money was one thing—to be made to look like fools by an ignorant country bumpkin like Cousin Milburn was more than we could stand.

By this time Sam had gotten out of the army. He wanted to go down and tear the TV studio up and perhaps get a little piece of Cous at the same time. Gussie and Eloise had other ideas. They didn't blame Cous as much as his wife Blondie, whom they thought had put him up to it. We went to the studio to try to find out what was going on, and Gussie and Eloise spotted Blondie prissing down the stairs from her dressing room. Blondie made the mistake of getting sassy with Eloise and before I knew it they were after her. She went flying back up the stairs screaming and shouting, "Milburn! Milburn! They're gonna kill me, Milburn." Fortunately she reached her dressing room first and locked the door.

We were fired from the show and even though a local merchant bought time and put us right back on, we could see that we were finished in Asheville. What we had thought was going to be our big break in show business broke us instead. We didn't know of anything else to do but pack up and head back to our big house in Evansville.

However, we suffered two additional disappointments. We had ordered a custom-made, nine-passenger Chrysler limousine—which we hoped to pay for with the money from the Cousin Milburn deal. It was to be painted a special color—Sam called it "Pepto-Bismol Pink." But when the car arrived in all its splendor, we had no money. The dealer finally sent it back to be repainted and sold somewhere else.

Times were hard. Nobody would come near us after what Cousin Milburn had said about us on TV. We were back on starvation rations, living on poke salad and egg sandwiches.

Our second disappointment came on our final tour together before we broke up. We already had more than two hundred thousand miles on our 1952 limousine and decided to use it on a last tour through South Carolina before heading back to Evansville. Gussie, Stella, Eloise, LaBreeska, Vestel, Vestel's sister, daddy, mama, Bobby, Sam, several nieces and nephews, and I climbed aboard the old limousine. Sam was driving and I was sitting in one of the little fold-up seats in the back when without warning a young kid, driving a souped-up roadster, smashed into the side of the car and knocked us into a ditch. Fortunately we were so tightly wedged into the car that no one was hurt, but the automobile was a wreck. We tied the doors shut with pieces of rags and completed the tour, but the end had come for the Goodman family singing group.

Returning to Evansville, we divided our spoils. Ruth had married and was living out of state. Rusty was still in the army. Sam went to work in a furniture factory, and the girls opened an upholstery shop. Bobby was working with a rock-'n'-roll combo, and Vestel and I went into evangelistic work. It was a sad day. Even though we were still living together in the big house, we felt like the end of the world had arrived.

Chapter Thirteen

In a crowd or alone, even far, far from home,
Reach out, touch the hand of the Lord.
On a busy thoroughfare, you can even find Him there,
Reach out, touch the hand of the Lord.
Touch the hand that was nailed to a cruel tree
A hand that has power, yet so tender it can be.
And when trouble assails you
This hand will never fail you,
Reach out, touch the hand of the Lord.

—RUSTY GOODMAN

In April, 1957, Vestel and I were invited to assist in a revival meeting in Madisonville, Kentucky, about sixty miles south of Evansville. David Epperson, an evangelist, was to do the preaching and he wanted us to help with the music. Rather than drive back and forth we rented a small house and moved down with the two young children.

At the close of the revival a Brother Lawrence Scaggs called on the phone. "Brother Howard, my wife and I would like for you and Brother Epperson to come around by the house tomorrow night. We have something we'd like to talk to you about."

That evening the Scaggs surprised us by saying, "We've just received nine thousand dollars in royalties from a coal mine. The Lord has laid it on our hearts to divide the tithe of this money between the two of you—four hundred fifty dollars apiece."

When I told Vestel about it after I got home, she gripped my arm squealing, "Oh, Howard, this little house we're living in

176

can be bought with a down payment of five hundred dollars. Do you reckon the Lord is telling us to settle down in Madisonville and start some kind of ministry here?"

We were beginning to see the Lord's hand in everything we did, so we agreed to pray seriously about the matter. The following day, however, David Epperson came by the house. "Brother Howard," he said, "I've been praying about this nine hundred dollars. I feel the Lord wants us to take all this money, invest it in a truck and a tent, and start traveling together in evangelistic work."

"Do you know where we could get a truck and tent for nine hundred dollars?" I asked.

"Yes, sir, the Lord has led me to a man who has an old truck and a big, three-pole tent that we can pick up at a bargain. I think God wants us to strike out on faith and hit the road for Him."

Of course, preaching and singing were the things I wanted to do more than anything else in the world. I turned and looked at Vestel. Her face was downcast and I could see that she had hoped we would remain in Madisonville. "You're my husband, Howard," she said in reply to my questioning. "I'll go wherever you go—even if I feel you're making a terrible mistake. Just 'going' and 'doing' is not always God's plan, though. Sometimes the Lord asks His people to stop and get to work where they are— rather than always looking for something big to do for Him. In this case I think you're dead wrong, and I feel that the Lord will show us that before very long."

There were times in the next few months when I wished desperately I had listened to Vestel that afternoon.

In the summer of 1957 we hit the road with our truck and tent as traveling evangelists. Gussie's daughter, LaBreeska, came along with us and the three of us often sang together.

Our first meeting was in Winnsboro, Louisiana. We set up our tent and had good crowds, but our expenses were so high we soon went in the hole financially. We pulled up the tent and moved it to Monroe.

Brother W. T. Hemphill was pastor of the Apostolic Pentecostal church in West Monroe, and we located the tent right across the road from the church. We held nightly meetings for two straight weeks before hurricane Audrey hit the Louisiana gulf coast and came swirling up the state. The little town of Cameron was almost wiped out and reports were that the heavy winds were raging northward through the state toward Monroe.

We woke the next morning to hear the radio say the hurricane was due to hit Monroe about noon. Forgetting about breakfast, we rushed out to try to save our tent and equipment. David and I were joined by Vestel and Sue (David's wife) and three men from the church. Vestel and Sue were folding chairs and laying them flat on the ground. David and the three men from the church helped me drag the organ out and load it on the truck so we could take it across the road to shelter. Just as we got the organ on the back of the truck David began to scream. "I hear it coming! I hear it coming! Everybody run!"

The sound of the wind roaring through the trees was like a hundred freight trains. The big tent filled with air like a giant balloon and the guy ropes that supported it from the outside snapped like threads. The hurricane wind swept under the tent, blasting it off the ground, and the canvas split open in a dozen places, ripping from side to side. The three huge poles that provided the main support and all the heavy ropes, cables, and pulleys surrounding the poles, came crashing down to the ground. The heavy canvas collapsed on top of it.

The wind screamed around the back of the truck as we tried to cover the organ. One of the men was picked up as if he were a leaf and blown off the back of the truck to the ground. All I could think of was Vestel, trapped under that tent, perhaps crushed to death by the poles and cables. Leaping off the truck, followed by Brother Epperson, we groped our way over the flapping canvas, prodding and feeling each bump to see if it were one of our wives.

Then the rain hit. Great bucketfuls of driving rain. It fell in sheets blocking our vision, but as we looked up we saw Vestel and Sue. They had escaped from the falling tent and climbed into David's car. The wind was blowing so hard they couldn't get the door closed and the rain was pouring in on them in great torrents.

Even though the wind destroyed the tent and sound system, it spared the truck and organ. We put the organ in the church building but left the tent and other ruined pieces of equipment right where they had fallen.

The downpour of rain was torrential, continuing throughout the next day and slackening off only in the afternoon. The depression which followed the storm seemed to move into Vestel's soul, for she began crying that afternoon and couldn't stop. "I just don't see how we can take much more," she said. "It seems that even God is against us."

I tried to comfort her, but her body was convulsed with great sobs. "It's just not fair, Howard," she cried. "All your life you've been trying to live for the Lord. Every place you've gone you've been unashamed of the gospel. People have ridiculed you, made fun of you, even tried to hurt you—but you've always stood firm. Now nature is against us. It's just not fair. Why doesn't God do something? Why doesn't He say something? Why has He turned His back on us like this?"

"Honey, maybe God's just letting all this happen to show us a miracle."

"Well, we're supposed to hold a service tonight. It'll take a miracle for Him to resurrect that old tent," Vestel sobbed. She pulled out of my grasp and ran out the front door into the drizzling rain. Reaching the car she crawled in the front seat, crying and praying.

I stood at the door, frustrated and helpless. All at once I was aware of old Brother Hemphill standing behind me. "Brother Howard," he said slowly, "do you believe that God is still on His throne?"

Without turning my head I answered, "I've never doubted it. Even if it rains forty days and forty nights and we lose everything we have, I'll not doubt Him. I say with Job, 'though He slay me, yet will I trust in Him.' "

"Amen," the old man said. Then he too quoted from Job. "The Lord gave, and the Lord hath taken away . . ." I joined him as we quoted the rest of the verse in unison . . . "blessed be the name of the Lord."

Brother Hemphill pushed past me out into the drizzling rain. He walked across the yard to where Vestel was sitting hunched over in the car. He pecked on the window and Vestel looked up. Surprised to see anyone out in the rain, she rolled the window down.

"How goes it, sister?" the old man asked.

Vestel began to sob even harder. "Oh, Brother Hemphill, God has turned His back on us. We invested every dime we had in that old tent because Brother Epperson said it was God's will. Now it's gone. God destroyed it. Why?"

The old man reached in and put his withered hand on Vestel's shoulder, patting her gently. "Daughter, it's the Lord. Let Him do what seems good to Him."

I stood in the door watching them and suddenly I heard Vestel shout, "Hallelujah!" The tears sprang to my eyes and ran down my face. I knew the victory had been won.

Brother Hemphill came back to the house, his face creased in smiles. "Tonight we'll just go in the church and finish the revival there. I'll get some spots on the radio so the folks will know we're still in business."

We still had a major problem, however. The PA system had been destroyed in the storm and there was no sound system in the church. This made little difference to me, but Vestel's voice was soft and very faint. It was impossible to hear her beyond the second row of pews unless she was singing directly into a microphone. I knew I could preach and sing without a microphone, but I also knew that Vestel could never be heard without amplification.

That night the little church building was jammed with people. As we entered, I turned to Vestel with a worried expression. "Honey, what are you going to do without a microphone?"

Vestel looked up at me, and I could see her face shining with the victory. "We'll just sing and forget it, even if they don't hear us past the first pew."

We took our seats on the front row, and Vestel began thumbing through the old paperback song book. She suddenly stopped flipping the pages and said, "Here's what the Lord wants me to sing tonight."

I looked at the hymn. It was entirely unfamiliar. "Have you ever sung it?" I said with a puzzled look. "I don't think I even know it."

"I don't know it either, so you better get up there and play it ahead of time. But the Lord told me to sing it."

The title of the song was "I Need No Mansions Here Below."

After Brother Hemphill opened the service, I played through Vestel's song so she could get the melody in her mind. Then she stood up on the platform, singing for the first time in her adult life without a microphone. The first notes that came from her mouth were incredible—indescribable. I'd never heard such a tremendous voice. It was the same Vestel, but she had her head back, her eyes closed as if in a trance, and the voice that came from her was the biggest, loudest, most heavenly voice I had ever heard. It was as if all the angelic trumpets were blowing at one time. The people were sitting with their mouths open in awe. Vestel just stood there, the music rolling out of her, with tears streaming down her face.

Revival broke out that night and continued for the next two weeks. More than fifty people received the baptism of the Holy Spirit before the week was out. The word spread like wildfire that miracles were breaking out in Brother Hemphill's church. People came from far and near to attend the services. The little church which seated only three hundred and fifty people was constantly jammed with more than four hundred each night.

On Tuesday night of the following week Brother Hemphill asked Vestel to preach. Whatever it was that happened out there in the car was still with her. I sat back in amazement as she preached under the anointing fire of the Holy Spirit.

That night after the service we sat in the kitchen of Brother Hemphill's modest home. "The victory's won," Vestel grinned. "I don't care what Satan throws at us from now on. I know whom I have believed and am persuaded that He is able to keep that which I have committed unto Him against that day." She was never to doubt God's goodness again.

There was another blessing that came from the revival. LaBreeska fell in love with Brother Hemphill's preacher-son Joel. It wasn't long after that when we lost a niece and gained a nephew.

As time passed, a series of circumstances developed which convinced us that we should separate from Brother Epperson. Instead of causing a stir, we let him have everything that was left of the original investment, packed our belongings, and returned to Evansville. We knew the Lord was directing us, but the way was still dim.

On the first of November I received a telephone call from the old pastor in Madisonville where we had held the meeting in April. "You know, Brother Goodman," he said, "I'm getting old and I'll be looking for someone to take my place before long. You're the best preacher I've heard. If you'll come down here and preach a revival that will last until Christmas, I might even want you to stay on and pastor this little church."

We agreed, and Vestel and I returned to Madisonville to conduct what we thought was going to be a month-long meeting. Vestel didn't say anything as we drove into town that afternoon, but I felt her snuggle up close to me. It wasn't necessary for her to say, "I told you so," for the Lord had already said it.

"Brother Goodman," the old pastor said the first night of the revival, "you just preach like the Lord leads. Preach it hard, 'cause these are hard folks and they need to have their feet stepped on."

I took him at his word. We had good crowds up until Wednesday night. Then things got slack, and I decided it was time to do some plain talking from the pulpit. "Some people love Lucy more than they love the Lord," I preached. "They've stayed home tonight to watch 'I Love Lucy' on TV rather than coming to church."

What I didn't know was that the old preacher's wife had stayed home to watch TV. The next night he got up and made a simple announcement. "The revival meeting will close tonight." No explanation was given. He just severed all relationship with us from that time. The only hint of the problem came when the pastor's wife refused to shake our hands at the door and said, "Haruumph!" as she walked by.

We prayed most of the night after the revival closed. We knew the Lord had a purpose in returning us to Madisonville, but this last setback just confused us. I knew the Lord had some plan in mind for us even though it was still unclear. I was up early the next morning walking the streets of Madisonville. Just off the square was an old theater building—the Cameo. It was boarded up and empty. I walked past it three or four times and each time the Lord said, "This is where I want you to begin my work."

I really thought the Lord had made a mistake. However, I began to ask around about the old building. Several families in the church, upset over the abrupt way we had been treated, had told me if I wanted to stay on in Madisonville and start a church they'd help. Taking them at their word I visited them, asking questions about the old Cameo Theater.

"Well, Brother Goodman," said one lady, "the only thing I know about that old place is that it's full of rats and roaches."

Another said, "I don't think it has any seats in it. The last I knowed they was using it to store refrigerators."

A third man told me, "Brother Howard, the man who owns that old building lives in Nashville. He hates preachers. Several have tried to rent it for a church, and he's just laughed at them."

I went back to the apartment and prayed with Vestel. As we prayed, Gideon's experience in the Old Testament came to mind. I recalled how Gideon used the lamb's fleece to make sure he knew God's will. So I decided to lay out my own kind of fleece.

"Lord," I prayed, "I've heard all kinds of stories about that old building. I've heard it's dirty and infested with rats and bugs. I've heard that the seats are all ripped out and that the man who owns it won't rent to preachers. Now Lord, I'm not asking you to do anything about the dirt, rats, and roaches. Me and Vestel can take care of that. But if it's your will for us to get that old building to start a church in, then I'm asking that you arrange for the seats to be in place and for you to touch the owner's heart so he'll rent it to us. If not, then we'll know this ain't your will."

I started to get up from my knees, but Vestel wasn't satisfied with my prayer. As she began to pray, I dropped back to my knees beside her. "Lord," Vestel prayed, "we feel that you have put us here in Madisonville for a purpose. I don't mind cleaning up dirt and trash. I've done that all my life. But Lord, you know I can't stand roaches—and rats scare me to death. So I'm laying out my own fleece. If you want us to have that old building then don't let it have any bugs or rats either. Hallelujah and Amen!"

That afternoon I called the theater owner in Nashville. "Yeah," he said. "I know you folks. I've heard you at the all-night singings in Ryman Auditorium. I'll be glad to rent that old building to you. I want one hundred fifty dollars a month and six months rent in advance."

I hung up the phone and turned to Vestel. "Well, praise the Lord. He'll rent it to us. Not only that but he says the seats are still in it. The only catch is he wants nine hundred dollars in advance."

Vestel grinned. "Why that's nothing. Our heavenly Father is rich. He owns the cattle on a thousand hills. Let's go down and see the building. We've got one more fleece to check out."

The owner had told us where we could pick up the key, and thirty minutes later we were inside the old theater. We walked slowly up and down the dark musky aisles. Cobwebs hung from the ceiling and the empty building echoed each step we took. Not only were all the seats in place, but they seemed to be almost brand new, although terribly dirty. Scraping away the dust and dirt we saw they were genuine leather upholstery with spring cushions—three hundred fifty-seven of them.

"Howard," Vestel said with an excited voice, "I don't see a single sign of rats or bugs, do you?"

She was right. Even though everything was covered by layers of dirt (the building had been boarded up for six years), there was no sign of rats or roaches. It was miraculous.

"Let's rent it! Let's rent it!" Vestel shouted with enthusiasm.

Holding up her hand, she said, "I can feel the hand of the Lord on us right now and in the name of Jesus Christ I claim this old building for Him."

It was noon the next day when I picked up the phone to call the owner. "We've decided to rent the theater," I said. "We'll sign a lease for six months, but we can't pay the full amount right now."

"All right, I'll take half the amount now and you can pay the balance as you go along."

"Praise the Lord," I shouted over the phone. "I'll mail you a check for four hundred fifty dollars this afternoon."

I hung up, turned, and looked at Vestel. Her eyes were sparkling with joy. It was good to be in the will of God.

We did have one small problem, however. We only had twenty dollars between us. However, we knew our Father could raise the money for us, so there were no feelings of anxiety. We both dropped to our knees and prayed, "Lord," I said, "it's almost 1:00 P.M. and the banks close at 4:00. I'm willing to give you every penny I have but that still leaves us four hundred thirty dollars short. Would you mind selling a few of those cows out there on your hills and arranging for us to get the balance so I can mail this man a check? After all, Lord, it's for your work."

The word spread quickly among some of the folks we knew. Brother Scaggs said, "Well, Brother Goodman, I've got the first two hundred dollars of it. I'd suggest you go by and see Sister Harris, too."

We walked to the home of Mrs. Clarence Harris. She opened the door saying, "Brother Goodman, I'm glad you came by. The Lord has just told me to give you one hundred dollars for your new church."

We walked back downtown and bumped into Bill Eppley on the street. "Brother Howard, I understand you're thinking about renting the old theater to start a church."

"That's right," I answered. "We're just waiting for the Lord to answer our prayers."

He reached in his pocket. "I'd like to be a part of the answer. Here's fifty dollars."

Before the bank closed I had gone to the teller's window and
bought a cashier's check for four hundred fifty dollars. Moments
later I put it in the mail, and we went back to our tiny apartment
praising God for his faithfulness.

That night, Vestel and I lay side by side in the darkness. The
only noise was the faint sound of music from a radio in the house
next door—playing Christmas carols. Vestel turned her head and
her hand touched mine. She softly began to quote a verse in
the Bible that had come to mean a great deal to both of us, "For
we know that all things work together for good to them that love
God, to them who are the called according to His purpose." She
paused, then continued. "You know, Howard, I've been lying
here thinking."

"About what, honey?" I said drowsily, my mind still running
through the miraculous happenings of the day.

"You know that four hundred fifty dollars that man wanted
for the rent on the theater?"

"Yes, I know."

"Well, that's the exact amount Brother Scaggs gave us back
in April. We went and spent it on that old tent. We knew at the
time the Lord wanted us to stay here, but we had gotten so used
to moving all the time we couldn't hold still."

I lay quietly, listening to the rustle of the covers in the other
room as Ricky and Vicki turned on the old couch where they
were sleeping. "I guess God had to let that hurricane come along
just to blow us back where he wanted us all along."

I felt Vestel's hand tighten around my fingers. "But ain't God
grand. If we hadn't gone off like that, even though we were out
of His will, my voice never would have changed. I'd still be singing in that little, soft voice."

I felt the tears coming to my eyes and running down the side
of my face to the pillow. "Not only that," I whispered, "He
scraped up another four hundred fifty dollars so we could do
what He wanted us to do all along—start a church here."

Vestel turned on her side and I felt her nuzzle her face up
against my neck. Gently she reached over and wiped away the
tears from my cheeks. "We don't have much of a church yet,"

she said. "We don't have any money. We don't have any people. All we've got is an old building that's six inches deep in dust."

I smiled slightly in the darkness. "And," I added, "we've got the Lord. If God is for us, who can be against us?"

Vestel sighed and draped her arm across my chest and shoulders, hugging me tightly to her. Outside the music of the little radio drifted through the cold Kentucky night, carrying the sounds up to where we rested above the old garage:

Joy to the world, the Lord is come,
Let earth receive her King.

Chapter Fourteen

It seems that I've sowed many a seed that's fell by the way,
For the birds to feed upon.
But I've held enough of the golden sheaves in my hand
To make me keep sowing on.

A cold wind was blowing stiffly and the scudding clouds over-head were deep gray when Vestel and I put the key in the padlock on the front door of the old Cameo Theater. "We've got two weeks before Christmas to get this place ready," I said as we stepped inside the cold, dingy lobby.

"We'll make it," Vestel answered laboring with several buckets and brooms. "Sister Scaggs, Sister Harris, and Sister Eppley are gonna meet me here. We're going to scrub this old building until it shines. Now you get out and start making some contacts with folks, letting them know that Life Temple is no longer a dream—that it's a reality."

It took two weeks to clean up the dirt, dust, and cobwebs. Using buckets of water and ammonia, the women washed down every seat. They got down on their hands and knees and not only scrubbed the carpets in the aisle, but under every seat as well.

"I bet there was twenty pounds of chewing gum under them seats," Vestel said on Friday night. "And look at my knees." She pulled up her skirt and showed me the big blisters on each knee where she had crawled across the concrete floor and down the aisle with her scrub brush.

"Well," I said, "the lights, water, and heat will be on next week. The Lord willing we'll have our first service New Year's Eve."

The Lord was willing, and we opened Life Temple on New Year's Eve, 1957, with a big singing and preaching meeting. That night all three hundred fifty-seven seats were filled for the service. We told the folks we'd have Sunday services and asked them to come back for Sunday school. Many of them did. We were on our way.

Sam, hearing of our new venture, came down from Evansville to help us get started. Even though he was driving back and forth from Evansville to Madisonville on the weekends, it looked like he was going to become part of the team. This became especially evident after he fell in love with Barbara Gibson.

Three months later Barbara's saintly old grandfather had a stroke. "If I thought my granddaughter would marry Sam Goodman, I'd die happy," he said. Barbara did marry Sam, and one week later her grandfather died—contented.

Sam moved to Madisonville and began to get serious about the Lord's work. "Howard," he said one afternoon, "I've got a vision about this church. I think God wants us to build a church where people can worship without respect to outward appearance. I think He wants a church where the emphasis isn't placed on what a person wears, whether he uses the right grammar, or whether he makes a lot of money. We're all poor folks ourselves, and I believe the Lord is leading us to build a poor folk's church."

Sam joined with us in the full ministry of the church, and we started singing together again. We were beginning to see evidences that the Lord was restoring our fractured family.

We were in the old theater a year and a half (the last six months we broadcasted a Sunday morning radio program over WFMW) when word came from the owner that he was going to sell the building. The only big place we could find on such short notice was a filthy building on the other side of the tracks that had been used as a pet shop. Once again Vestel and her

women went to work with scrub brushes and ammonia to try
to clean up the smelly old building.

"Howard," Vestel said after coming home with a new set of
blisters on her knees, "I sure wish we'd put our rat and roach
fleece back out before renting that old building. If another one of
those horrid creatures runs across my hand while I'm scrubbing
floors, I think I'll pack up and go back to Sand Mountain."

"Besides," she added, "I ain't so sure there's not other varmints
living in there. I think I'd die if a snake slithered out of one of
those holes in the wall."

I patted her shoulder. "It's not all bad, honey. The owner of
the theater called me on the phone today and offered to sell me
all the old seats for a dollar apiece."

"That's three hundred fifty-seven dollars we've got to get from
some place," Vestel said.

"We've been able to save up fifty-seven dollars ourselves. All
we need is three hundred more. I've been thinking about going
to a bank to try to borrow it."

"What bank do you think would loan money to folks like us?"
Vestel asked honestly. "Our offerings at the church are running
about fifty dollars a week and we're living on a thirty-dollar-a-
week budget. Now we've lost our building and are having to
move into an old dog house. I don't think there's a bank that
would loan us three dollars, much less three hundred."

Vestel was right about one thing. From man's point of view,
things looked bleak. However, we had learned that God's ways are
always higher than man's ways. So we agreed to pray about the
matter for three days before we did anything.

On the morning of the fourth day we were sitting at the breakfast table, and I looked over at Vestel. "It's been three full days.
We haven't mentioned it a single time. What do you think?"

Vestel said, "Honey, the only answer I get is to go to the
Kentucky Bank and Trust Company and ask for a loan."

"That's the answer the Lord gave me, too," I said as a feeling
of relief swept over me.

"You go to the bank as soon as breakfast is over," Vestel said.
"The children and I will stay here and pray."

I walked into the Kentucky Bank and Trust Company an hour later and introduced myself to Mr. L. K. Bell, the president. "Oh, yes, I know who you are," he said as he looked me over sternly. "I've heard your radio program on Sunday morning."

"Praise the Lord," I said.

"What's that? What did you say?" Mr. Bell asked.

"Oh, I was just thanking God that He introduced me to you before I got here."

"Indeed He did," Mr. Bell said. "Yes, sir, I know all about you, and before I ask you why you're here, I want to say something."

My mouth was dry and my heart began to beat hard in my chest. "Y-y-yes, sir," I stuttered.

"You're the strangest Pentecostal preacher I've ever heard, and I've heard a lot of them," Mr. Bell said looking me straight in the eye.

My spirits dropped. I felt a big lump gathering in the pit of my stomach and moving up into my throat. Had I made a mistake in coming to this man? Had I misunderstood the will of God? Why would God want to subject me to more humiliation when all I was trying to do was be His servant? All these questions raced through my mind as I tried to keep my jaw from quivering in disappointment. "I don't understand," I said in a weak voice. "What do you mean?"

"I mean," said Mr. Bell as he seated himself behind his big desk, "that you're the first Pentecostal preacher I've ever heard that sounded like you may think some of us Presbyterians might know Jesus Christ. I like that in a man. Now, Brother Goodman," he said, emphasizing the word *Brother,* "what can we do for you?"

The bank agreed to lend us the needed three hundred dollars and we began to move the seats out of the theater into the old pet shop. It was then we encountered another problem. The old building would only accommodate two hundred of the seats. No more.

That evening I told Vestel. "I'm afraid I've made a horrible mistake. I bought all those seats and now we don't have anything to do with them. We've got to get them out of the theater by the end of the week, but we haven't any place to store them."

"Now listen, Howard," Vestel said as she cleared the dishes from the table and put them in the tiny little sink, "God doesn't waste anything. He knew what He was doing when He told us to buy all them seats. Let Him worry about it—not you."

I went into the front room and lay down on the couch. Less than ten minutes later I was disturbed by a knock at the front door. It was the pastor of the Lighthouse Mission, another little church in town.

"Brother Goodman, do you have any of those seats you'd like to sell?"

My heart was in my throat as I answered, "I've got one hundred and fifty that you could have."

"What will you take for them?"

"Well, Brother Daniel," I said, "you know I gave a dollar apiece for those seats."

"That's right," he answered.

"Then you also know I ain't gonna take that for them."

"I figured that," he smiled.

"I'll take two dollars a seat for them."

He never blinked an eye. "Well, we'll take them. I'll bring you a check the first thing in the morning for three hundred dollars."

"Just make it out to the Kentucky Bank and Trust Company," I said. "We have a little debt down there we'd like to pay off."

We moved into the old pet shop and began church services. Things were hectic, however. We had been having capacity crowds in the theater, but the folks were reluctant to crowd into the smelly old building. It was hot that summer and the lack of ventilation made things that much worse. To top it all off, the first Sunday in the pet shop a giant highland terrapin that had, as Vestel suspected, been hiding in the woodwork, came crawling down the aisle right during the middle of my sermon. He was as big in diameter as the steering wheel of a Mack truck and crawled the entire length of the aisle while I preached. I tried my best to keep my eyes off him, but they were drawn as if by magnets to that stupid turtle who kept inching his way forward toward the pulpit. People were standing up all over the room trying to see what I was looking at. The ladies on the aisle were trying to keep from screaming while they held their feet high off the floor, attempting at the same time to keep their knees covered. By the time the turtle reached the altar rail, the church service had broken up; some people were screaming in fright and others were laughing hilariously.

"The least you could have done was baptize him, preacher," one wag said at the door after the service was over.

"Baptize him nothing," I said. "I've got him in a box behind the pulpit. I'm going to take him home and eat him."

Three months in the pet shop in the middle of the summer, however, were more than we could take. Every Sunday the temperature got hotter and the smell got worse. We began praying in earnest that God would intervene.

He did. Around the first of September we heard that the congregation of the Church of Christ had built a new building and parsonage on the other side of town. They were vacating their old buildings on Grapevine Road. But when we contacted the real estate agent and he quoted us a price of twenty-five thousand dollars, we shook our heads in despair. "That's just too much," I said. "We'll have to wait until God opens some other door."

But it seemed the only door that was open was the back door of the church. We were losing our members quicker than we were getting them. They just couldn't stand the heat and the smell. Again Vestel and I started praying.

Two weeks later I received a call from J. W. Hatchel, the chairman of the board of trustees of the Church of Christ. "Preacher," he said, "we've taken the building out of the hands of the real estate agent, and we're going to quote you our bottom-dollar price for the church and parsonage. We'll let you have both buildings for nineteen thousand dollars."

I thought about the little white stucco church building with the pretty auditorium and the basement rooms which had been used for Sunday school. Next to it was a large parking lot and a four-room parsonage which would be ten times better than our garage apartment. "Okay, give me a chance to talk it over with the church people Sunday," I said.

"We'll take forty-five hundred down and the rest at one hundred fifty dollars a month."

"I haven't the slightest idea how we can raise forty-five hundred dollars," I said dejectedly, "but we'll see."

Next Sunday I told the folks about it. Our congregation had dwindled to about seventy-five persons since we'd left the theater. I knew if we stayed in the pet shop much longer they would all be gone. Some even said they were beginning to itch, even though the place had been thoroughly disinfected.

"If you'll give me two thousand dollars cash, I believe the Lord will open up a way so we can buy the church," I said. "I'll tell you this. I won't lose your money. I'll make it safe."

Mr. E. W. Jackson, who owned a real estate agency in town, was the first to stand up. "Preacher, Sister Jackson and I will give you five hundred dollars toward the purchase of a new church building."

That started the ball rolling. Another man pledged one hundred dollars. Others did the same. Some gave ten dollars, and some only a dollar. Within minutes nearly everyone present had pledged something. We totaled the amount and it added up to seventeen hundred dollars. Mr. Jackson was back on his feet. "I'll give the last three hundred to the glory of God."

Monday morning I called Mr. Hatchel on the phone. "I collected two thousand dollars yesterday."

"That's fine, Brother Goodman," he said. "If you give me the money we'll hold the property for you and give you time to raise the other twenty-five hundred before you move in."

I said, "Mr. Hatchel, I'm going to be fair with you. You know where we're meeting down there in that old dog house. You know what kind of shape it's in. I've raised the last two thousand dollars I can raise in that dump. If you'll let us give you two thousand now and move into the new church building, I'll pay you five hundred dollars a month for the next five months. Then we can enter into a straight contract at one hundred fifty dollars per month. But if you don't let us take possession now, I'll never be able to raise the rest of the money for you."

"I'll have to talk to the board," he said. "I'll call you back later."

In less than an hour the phone rang. "Brother Goodman, we'll accept your proposition."

I hung up and turned to Vestel. Her eyes were twinkling. "Now where in the world are you going to get five hundred dollars per month, Howard Goodman? Our church isn't raising fifty dollars per week, and we've got to have something to live on ourselves."

I reached over and pulled her close to me so the top of her head tucked in under my chin. "I'll tell you how I'm gonna do it," I said. "I'm going out on one of those thousand hills owned by the Lord and sell some cattle."

The next week our congregation worshiped in the little white church building on Grapevine, and Vestel, Ricky, Vicki, and I moved into the parsonage next door. Over the next five months the church raised the five hundred dollars per month, with enough to spare to keep us in groceries at the same time.

* * * *

There's a footnote that needs to be added here. Two days before we moved into the new church building, Mr. Hatchel called me back. "Brother Goodman, I have something else I want to talk to you about."

I was scared. I didn't know what he wanted and was afraid he might be getting ready to back down on his agreement. He said, "Do you have your own seats?"

I said, "Yes sir, we have two hundred of them."

"That would just about fill the little church," he said. "The reason I'm calling is that our new church needs some seats for the basement. If you'll let us move our old slat seats out of the auditorium, we'll knock another five hundred dollars off the price of the building."

That night Vestel figured that our original investment of fifty-seven dollars had netted the church more than ten times that amount in cash—and we still had our genuine leather, spring upholstery seats to go in our new place of worship.

Chapter Fifteen

Won't you come along with me and go
To the land where milk and honey flow.
I ain't hesitatin', I know my Saviour's waitin' for me.
He'll say enter in my child, a job well done;
Fought a good fight, now your race is run;
And it'll all be over but the shoutin' when we get home.

It'll all be over but the shoutin';
All the joys of Heaven I'm a countin'.
It'll all be over but the shoutin' when we get home.
Only thirty minutes of silence you'll hear.
Then we're gonna shout for a million years
And it'll all be over but the shoutin' when we get home.

—RUSTY GOODMAN

Daddy died in October 1959 in the Veterans Hospital in Louisville. He had moved down to Madisonville with us and seemed so proud of our new church, but at the age of ninety he fell and broke his hip. We took him to the hospital in Louisville and he never came home.

We decided to have the funeral in the cemetery outside the little church in Burnwell where Uncle Herschel still preached. There daddy would be laid to rest in the Alabama sand out of which he had scratched a living for all those years.

Vestel and I drove down the day before the funeral and stayed overnight with Uncle Herschel and Aunt Flossie in the little house on the hill that daddy helped build.

I slept little that night. When the dawn had come and the sun crept over the black pines on the hills to the east, I got out of bed and sat in a chair facing the window. Laying my tired head on my arm I looked longingly at the Alabama countryside that spread out before me. It was the same familiar scene I remembered as a boy, only now scattered houses and the strange intrusion of a paved road shattered the memory. Looking out over the old chinaberry trees daddy had planted when I was a boy, I could see Yerkwood Mountain in the distance. Everything was fresh and dewy and silent and green. The sight of the little church steeple through the trees brought a measure of balm and comfort to my broken heart.

Alabama at sunrise. The squatty log chicken house was clay daubed against rats and weasels and clean with whitewash. The garden with its rows of corn, bright yellow squash, butter beans, and turnips was weeded and neatly fenced with split-oak rails. The rising sun reflected with faint glistening off the red of the tomatoes hidden deep inside the green leaves of their vines. They were ready for picking and it wouldn't be long before Aunt Flossie would be busy canning, making pickles in the old churn crocks in the cellar, and shelling corn for the winter. The ducks and chickens were waddling and strutting off toward the little creek that wound its lazy way through the field below the house, for under the bushes and near the water's edge would be found the choicest worms and slugs. The only sound was the soft cooing of a mourning dove in the distant field and the rat-a-tat-tat of a woodpecker hammering away at an old hollow tree near the window.

I turned and looked at Vestel, just rousing from the troubled night's sleep. Our eyes met and instantly mine filled with tears. Turning quickly I looked long and deep at the rose-colored sky that was fast turning to light blue.

I heard her rise and walk barefooted across the wooden floor to where I was sitting. I felt her nearness behind me, her body still warm from the bed. She laid her hands gently on my shoulders.

"I'll miss him," I said in a choked voice. "He loved this earth and the feel of the red clay under his feet. He loved to watch the maples and dogwoods burst into new life in the spring. He loved to walk through the woods in the fall, scuffing the fallen leaves with his feet and watching the sun stream through the half-naked trees and bring life to the earth below. He loved to take us fishing in the summer, and sometimes would hide behind a big tree and scare me and Gussie into thinking he'd gone off someplace and left us all alone."

I paused, as the waves of nostalgia swept across my heart. "I remember one time we were fishing down at the pond near grandpa's place. Gussie and I had little old stick poles with strings tied to the ends and bent pins for hooks. We looked up and daddy was gone. I can still remember that horrible empty feeling. Gussie began to scream at the top of her little voice, 'Daddy! Daddy! It's Gussie Mae and Willie Howard. It's Gussie Mae and Willie Howard! Come back! Come back!'

"Daddy poked his head out from behind a big old elm where he was hiding and grinned. We dropped our old stick poles and went running to him, our bare feet leaping over rocks and logs. We jumped into his arms and hugged his neck so tight we pulled him over on the ground on top of us . . ."

My voice faltered and broke as I looked with tear-filmed eyes at the peaceful scene out the window toward Yerkwood Mountain. I felt Vestel's soft arms encircle my neck and shoulders as she stood behind me.

There was a long moment of deep silence as we both watched the sun rise higher in the sky. The shadows disappeared on the mountain. "There's a little boy inside all of us," I said. "No matter how old we get. No matter how much money we make. No matter how far away from home we may wander or how deep into sin we fall, there is still a little boy that cries out for a daddy's loving arms."

I felt my arms going up, extending above my head and heard myself saying, "Oh, praise the Lord. . . . I can feel the loving arms of my heavenly Father encircling me with His love."

That afternoon, standing at the side of the open grave, we listened as Uncle Herschel read from the old Bible. "For I am now ready to be offered, and the time of my departure is at hand.

I have fought a good fight, I have finished my course, I have kept the faith: Henceforth there is laid up for me a crown of righteousness, which the Lord, the righteous judge, shall give me at that day: and not to me only, but unto all them also that love his appearing."

The simple casket was slowly lowered into the Alabama countryside. People turned to leave, but the family lingered by the grave, savoring those last few precious moments before separation, not quite willing to turn loose of that which God said was no longer ours. We stood silently, surrounded by our wives and children, all of whom loved daddy as much as we did.

It was mama, her hair now silver gray, who broke the silence. "You children remember those old days at the tabernacle over there in the woods. Your daddy had accepted Christ as his Savior, but wasn't quite sure about worshiping in the Spirit. Remember how he used to stand at the back of the tabernacle, half in the light and half in the darkness, watching what was going on at the altar rail?"

We nodded, remembering.

Mama continued. "Well, children, your daddy has now stepped out of the darkness into the full circle of light. Today he's worshiping in a tabernacle not made with hands, singing praises to God Almighty in the power of the Holy Ghost. Today your daddy's shoutin' around the throne—and so am I."

Throwing her head back mama put her hands in the air and shouted through the tears, "Hallelujah! Praise the Lord!"

The victory was hers. And ours too—because of Jesus.

Chapter Sixteen

If there's a special need within your life, my friend,
And you're seeking for an answer day by day,
If by faith you'll start believing;
Mighty soon you'll be receiving,
For the answer is already on the way. *

—RUSTY GOODMAN

Rusty was discharged from the army before we left Evansville. True to his threat, he did not return to the group. Instead he moved to Nashville where he made connections with Martha Carson, who was singing with the Grand Old Opry. He joined her troup, played rhythm guitar, and acted as the master of ceremonies on stage.

Martha decided she had outgrown the Opry and moved her troup to New York to try for the big time. Rusty, sensing that success and stardom were almost within his reach, joined the crowd on Broadway with their cocktails, cigarettes, and wild parties.

But Rusty wasn't cut from this kind of mold, and it wasn't long before he knew he had to make a decision: either commit himself to secular music or break from it entirely. Therefore, despite the prospect of an appearance on the Ed Sullivan show and a three-week engagement at Lake Tahoe, Rusty decided to quit the troupe and come home.

* "The Answer's on the Way" by Charles Goodman © 1964 Reico Music Publishers, Inc. Used with permission of the publisher; all rights reserved.

We had just finished supper when the phone rang. I answered it. Rusty was crying so hard I could hardly understand him. "Howard, I'm so miserable. I've just gotta come home. You folks pray for me. I've never been so burdened in all my life."

We did pray. Two nights later Rusty was home. It was a glad, glad reunion.

Singing, however, was the number one love in Rusty's life and the family just wasn't singing much at all. Therefore, when Eastmon Napier of the Plainsmen Quartet called Rusty from Dallas, Texas, and asked him to join their group as the baritone singer, Rusty accepted. After his experience with the night clubs in New York he welcomed the prospect of singing gospel music. But it wasn't long before he was trapped in the same kind of worldly life he had tried to escape while in New York, only this time it was in the insidious trappings of gospel singing.

Despite his kind of life it was obvious that Rusty was destined for big things in gospel music. Critics acclaimed him equal to or better than Tennessee Ernie Ford.

The big break came for the Plainsmen when Jimmie Davis, former governor of Louisiana and popular gospel singer, called from Shreveport. "Boys," Jimmie drawled, "I need some help. I'm doing a couple of church dates over here at Shreveport, and I'll pay you a hundred dollars a night if you'll come and back me up while I'm singing."

One hundred dollars a night was big money for the Plainsmen, and before long they were regulars with Jimmie Davis as he stumped the state of Louisiana.

Rusty didn't realize it at the time, but this was Jimmie's method of running for governor. He called it "preconvention campaigning." His smooth style of singing and talking nearly always swayed the audience in his favor. "If I could," he would say to an audience in a little country church, "this is the thing I would like to do all the rest of my life. It would take all my time, but this is where my heart is and one of these days I'm gonna cut loose from all my ties and just visit churches all over this great land."

Then the big announcement came. Jimmie called Rusty and

the Plainsmen into his big home in Shreveport. All the big names
in Louisiana music were there too. They stood around the
palatial living room while Jimmie talked.

"Boys," Jimmie said, rubbing his ear, "I've called you all in
here to tell you that we're gonna do this thing." (He never did
say he was going to run for governor.) "I want you to help me.
We're gonna put you all on salary—five hundred dollars per
month. It won't be much, but you can buy some beans and still
have a few dollars left over to go in your pocket. If we win, I'm
gonna give every man a one-thousand-dollar bonus."

So from Pilottown to Potash, from Mamou to Mer Rouge, from
Bougalusa to Natchitoches, Rusty, the Plainsmen, the fiddlers,
the banjo players, and the country singers stumped the state with
Jimmie Davis. Every place they went it was the same—fried
shrimp, oysters, fast music, and political speeches that sounded
more like revival sermons. Jimmie was opposed by the big machine from Orleans Parish as well as by the Long machine
masterminded by Uncle Earl himself. His campaign was at the
grassroots, and his political speeches were meant to touch the
minds and hearts of the folks who lived there.

"I've promised myself and you that I'd conduct this campaign
in a clean way, and I've got to live with Jimmie Davis whether I
win or lose," he would say.

"I feel this way 'cause one of these days they're gonna take me,
like they're gonna take you, out to some silent city on a hill.
There six feet of earth's waiting for you and waiting for me. The
great equalizer is out there and there's no big Is and no little
yous. All men are the same size. And when that day comes, I
want them to be able to look on old Jimmie and say, 'Well, old
Jimmie might not have had all the answers, but he didn't claim
to have them either. He did his best, and you can't ask a man
for more than that.' Thank you, friends, for listening. God bless
you."

With such an appeal Jimmie Davis won the election. A short
time later Rusty and the other Plainsmen moved from Dallas to
Baton Rouge to go to work for the new governor of Louisiana.

It was a year later when Vestel, Sam, and I were invited to

sing and preach in the Kansas City Camp Meeting of the Pente-costal Church of God. While we were there, Rusty called and said the Plainsmen would pay us one hundred dollars if we'd drive over to Wichita and sing with them in a concert. We met Rusty at the door of the hotel that afternoon and smelled whiskey on his breath. He looked horrible.

That night after the concert Vestel approached Rusty back-stage. He was smoking a big cigar and laughing loudly with some of the other singers. He looked up and saw her coming. "Now, Vestel," he said defiantly, with a cutting edge in his voice, "don't come at me with your preaching. I've heard just about as much of that stuff as I can stand. I don't want to hear any more—from you or anyone else."

Vestel cried all the way back to Kansas City that night.

The next afternoon I preached under the big, open pavilion at the camp meeting. It was hot and there was little breeze blow-ing. The people were all in shirt sleeves, and many of them were waving little fans to try to stir up some air. My text was Judges 11:30, "Jephthah vowed a vow to the Lord," and my subject was, "If you make a vow to the Lord, keep it." During the sermon I related an incident in my childhood when I had made such a vow. It was when Rusty was a baby and had developed a serious sickness. Mama insisted we take him to the old tabernacle to be healed. I carried him down the aisle and held him up before the altar rail. "Lord," I prayed, "you gave him to us and you have the right to take him back. But if you will heal him, I will serve you the rest of my life."

The Lord did heal Rusty, and I went ahead to tell the congre-gation how that vow had helped keep me in the ministry, even when times were mighty rough.

While I was preaching, Vestel received a special message from God. "My daughter, I want you to write a letter to Rusty. Do not delay. Do it now. Seal it and at the close of the service carry it to the pulpit. The preachers will lay hands on it and pray. If you are obedient to me then one year from today Rusty will be in this same camp meeting, saved and filled with the Holy Spirit."

Vestel grabbed a pad out of her purse and wrote furiously while

I finished my sermon. At the close of the service Brother A. J.
Thomas, the Kansas state superintendent of the Pentecostal
Church of God, came to the platform to ask if there were any
closing announcements. I looked up and saw Vestel coming
down the aisle. "Yes, sir," she said, "the Lord told me to write
this letter and ask the preachers to pray over it before I mail it."

Brother Thomas reached out, took the letter, and gently laid
it on the altar rail. He asked all the preachers to come forward. A
huge group gathered at the altar. As many as could, reached
forward and laid hands on the letter. The rest put a hand on the
backs of those in front of them, lifted the other hand toward
heaven, and joined in praying while Brother Thomas asked the
Holy Spirit to anoint the letter.

God was working in other ways also. Rusty had met a pretty
little blond from El Dorado, Arkansas. A year after they were
married their first child, Tanya, was born. Between his wife,
Billie, and little Tanya, the Holy Spirit at last had a voice in
Rusty's life. Our prayers and Vestel's letter were just part of the
big overall plan of God to return Rusty Goodman to the fold.

In October 1962, the phone rang in the parsonage. I picked it
up and shouted for Vestel. "Honey, get on the extension. It's
Rusty. He's in some kind of trouble."

"Howard," he said, "I've gone just about as far as I can."

I thought he was in financial trouble and calling for help.
"Rusty, all I've got in the world is a ten-dollar bill."

"No, no, it's not that." I could tell he was crying on the other
end of the wire. "Billie and me have got to get back to the Lord.
We need help. I've been out on the road singing with the Plainsmen and the radio says the Cuban crisis will explode any moment. Howard, we're not ready to die. We want help and we
want it now."

"What do you want us to do?" I asked.

"I called up Joel and LaBreeska in Bastrop. They weren't there,
but I talked with Mrs. Hemphill. Joel's preaching a revival in
Winnsboro, and we're gonna drive up there tonight and go to

church with them. But," he added, "we want you all to come down and pray for us."

"Rusty, I don't know how in the world we can come down there," I said. "This ten dollars is all I've got and it ain't near enough money to even buy gas."

Just then I heard Vestel's voice on the other phone. "Rusty, we'll be there."

"But you don't have any money."

"We'll get it," Vestel said confidently. "If God provided a whale to get Jonah to Nineveh, he can provide us gas to get to Louisiana."

I hung up and Vestel walked back into the room. "Let's get packed," she said. "God's moving in a hurry."

I was putting the suitcases in the trunk of the car and wondering where we were going to get the money to buy gas when the phone rang. Vestel picked it up. "Sister Goodman," a woman's voice said, "this is Lucille Welch. I guess you know I'm not much of a tither at church, but I was praying just a minute ago and the Lord spoke to me. He said you needed twenty dollars. I don't know what it's for, but I've got it here at the house. If you can't come by and pick it up, I'll bring it over."

"Praise God!" Vestel shouted. "Honey, you wait right there. We're on our way out of town and will stop by and pick it up as we leave."

In the meantime, Rusty, still in Baton Rouge, had called Jimmie Davis. He was supposed to rehearse with him at the mansion that night for a record they were going to cut. "I'm sorry, governor," Rusty said, "but the Lord has more authority than even you. He's told me to go to church tonight and I don't know when I'll be back."

"Rusty," the governor drawled, "I take orders from the Lord too. If he's telling you to do something, do it. I'll be praying for you."

The little church where Joel and LaBreeska were ministering was the same one that had sponsored us when we put up our tent in Winnsboro several years before. When Rusty and Billie drove up in the church yard, Joel rushed out and met them.

Throwing his arms around Rusty and Billie, he said, "Mother called me from Bastrop. I prayed you'd come."

At the close of the service Joel gave an altar call. Rusty leaned over and touched Billie's hand. She was crying and they both got up, went to the altar, and knelt for prayer. Some of the folks from the congregation gathered around them, laying on hands and praying. The restoring work of God was just about completed.

Vestel and I drove all night and arrived in Baton Rouge the next day. We spent the next two days in prayer and Bible study with Rusty and Billie. Rusty had arranged with the pastor of the First Assembly of God Church in Baton Rouge for me to preach on Sunday. At the close of the service Rusty and Billie presented themselves as candidates for water baptism.

It was glorious. We went up to the baptistry where I had the privilege of lowering my own brother under the baptismal waters. Billie, who had been raised in a Baptist church, followed Rusty into the pool. As she came up out of the water, her face was shining with a heavenly glow and her lips were praising God with a heavenly language. I could almost hear the flutter of the wings of the dove as the Spirit filled her soul.

Rusty stayed with the Plainsmen several more months, but the pressure became increasingly heavy. After a tour where the group sang with a young country and western singer who was just beginning to achieve recognition, Johnny Cash, Rusty came home and announced to Billie, "Honey, I've just quit the quartet."

That Sunday night we received a phone call. "We've got everything packed in a big U-Haul trailer," Rusty said excitedly. "The trailer hitch is scraping the highway, but the Lord willing we'll be with you all in the morning."

That evening as Rusty and Billie left Baton Rouge, the big trailer lumbering along behind them, they pulled over to the side of the road just beyond the city limits. Joining hands in the front seat they both prayed. "Dear God," Rusty said, "we're giving You ourselves. Like Lot leaving Sodom, we pray for strength that we won't ever look back. Protect us. Help us. Use us."

As they pulled out into the four-lane highway, Billie asked, "Rusty, what *are* you going to do after you get to Madisonville?"

"I don't know," he said, "I just want to help in the church some little way. Maybe I can play the organ."

"Play the organ?" Billie said, sitting up straight and looking at Rusty in amazement. "You can't play the organ. You've never played one in your entire life. You can't even play the piano. All you can play is the guitar."

She sighed and slumped back down in the seat. "Besides," she said as an afterthought, "they don't even have an organ at that church."

Billie was right, but she was underestimating the power of God not only to instruct—but to provide.

Rusty, Billie, and Tanya pulled into the church parking lot at 7:00 A.M. We had hardly had a chance to greet them when a big music van backed into the same parking lot and stopped at the door of the church.

"What's this?" Rusty asked.

"Well, we went out and bought an organ last week," I said.

"But you don't have anyone in the church who can play," Rusty said. "Are you going to play it?"

"Oh no, not me," I laughed. "I sound like a circus coming to town when I play. We just got a good buy on the instrument and I figured the Lord would send somebody along to play it."

Rusty stood there in the parking lot between the church and the parsonage and cried. He was tired from having driven all night, but these were not tears of exhaustion. They were tears of rejoicing. The Lord had confirmed their decision with signs and wonders.

The next day Vestel, Sam, and I left for Kansas City and the camp meeting. Rusty went along as an answer to prayer.

The following Sunday Rusty was at the organ in our little church. His music was pretty crude to begin with, but it didn't take him long to pick it up. With his natural ability he soon mastered the chords and pedals and became a good organist.

Until they were able to rent a small house, Rusty, Billie, and Tanya slept on the basement floor of the church building. We invited Rusty to go with us that weekend to a small Methodist church for a Sunday afternoon concert. He sang with us and his share of the offering was six dollars. He tried to give it back but we made him take it. He had used up his money and that was all he had to try to support his wife and child. Things looked pretty dark.

The next afternoon Rusty went upstairs from where he was sleeping and living in the basement of the little church and sat down at the organ. He was alone in the auditorium for several hours and it was dark when I heard him leave the church and start across the parking lot toward our house.

Rusty sat down in our living room and talked quietly as I listened. "When we came up here, God promised me He'd supply all my needs. I went over there in that auditorium and played the organ some this afternoon. Then I climbed down off the bench and got on my knees and prayed, 'Lord, You're gonna have to show me what to do because we're out of money and out of food. We don't have anything.'"

Rusty got up and walked toward the door, looking out toward the little white church that reflected in the dim street lights. "Do you know what the Lord told me, Howard?" he said. "The Lord said it so clearly I could almost hear it. He said, 'The answer's on the way.'"

Rusty reached into his hip pocket and pulled out a sheet of paper upon which he had jotted some notes and words. "I got up from my knees and climbed back on the organ bench and began to play and sing. These words and notes just flowed from my mouth. After I sang it through the first time, I took a pencil and wrote it down." He handed the sheet to me.

I reached up and turned on the floor lamp. Bending over I could barely make out the words and notes on the paper.

Many times I've bowed beneath a heavy load
And on bended knees to God a prayer I'd pray;
As I knelt there on the floor,
He'd remind me just once more
That the answer was already on the way.

Oh yes, the answer's on the way this I know.
Jesus said it, I believe it and it's so.
Our Heavenly Father knows the need before we pray;
And we can rest assured the answer's on the way.

The following morning a letter arrived for Rusty. Enclosed was a check for fifteen hundred dollars and a note from Jimmie Davis in Louisiana stating that this was money he owed Rusty for past services. It had been mailed day before yesterday. The answer *was* on the way.

Chapter Seventeen

Oh! Had it not been for a place called Mount Calv'ry,
Had it not been for the old rugged cross;
Had it not been for a Man called Jesus,
Then forever my soul would be lost.

—RUSTY GOODMAN

Many times, in the years that followed, I looked back on those miraculous answers to prayer and received strength to keep pushing on. As the psalmist remembered God's ability to bring His people through the Red Sea and to the Promised Land, so I gained strength day by day in "forgetting not all His benefits."

Such a strength was needed for the days that lay ahead. We wanted to sing together as a family, but the opportunities were limited and the field highly competitive. Thus when WLTV went on the air in Bowling Green, about seventy miles from Madisonville, Rusty suggested we apply for time.

"Howard," he said, "we ought to go over there and audition. They don't have any network affiliation and someone said they were crying for talent."

I shook my head. "Rusty, you weren't with us when we had that terrible experience in Asheville with Cousin Milburn. If that's what we're gonna get into with TV, I just don't want any part of it."

The next afternoon we were sitting in my living room watching TV. Rusty got up to switch channels when the announcer said, "If you have talent, or you know of anyone who does, and you would like to appear on TV—contact the program director at this station: WLTV, channel 13, Bowling Green."

Rusty turned and looked at me, his eyes wide as saucers. "Howard, we're going over there tomorrow. That was a message from God."

"Aw, they won't give us no program," I said.

"Those folks need talent," Rusty said, "I say we ought to go."

Sam and Vestel agreed. The following afternoon we piled in the car and drove over to Bowling Green. Rusty went in and cornered the program director. "I want you to see and hear the Happy Goodman Family," he said. "They can really sing."

We were herded into a studio and I sat down at a piano which was smaller than I was. The program director gave us a signal from the control booth and I hit a couple of hot licks on the piano and we went into "Born to Serve the Lord." When we finished, a voice from the control booth said, "Give me about five minutes and I'll be with you."

In less than a minute the director was back in the studio. "When can you start a regular program? What nights would you like to have?"

A week later we started a regular thirty-minute Monday-night show over WLTV. Since it was a live show we had to drive over every week, but we didn't mind the inconvenience because almost immediately invitations began to pour in asking us to sing in various concerts around the state. It looked like we were back in business.

"Howard," Rusty said to me one afternoon as we were standing in the parking lot, "if we're gonna start singing, we've got to have a better sound system. This little old amplifier and loud speaker just can't handle what we're capable of putting out. Things are changing. The Lord let me stay down there with the Plainsmen long enough to realize that if singing groups don't update their equipment and start using modern methods they'll never make it professionally."

I glanced at Rusty. He was standing beside me, kicking the loose white gravel at his feet. "Rusty, I don't object to progress.

I'm just afraid as soon as we start changing our methods, we'll water down our message."

Rusty walked over to the back of my old car and with his finger traced designs on the dust of the trunk. "Howard, when I was in New York, I tried to get those folks to use some gospel music. I knew it would go over big. They finally agreed to sing 'Satisfied.' Only when they got to the line, 'I'm gonna sit down beside my Jesus,' they changed it to 'I'm gonna sit down by my Maker.' The song flopped and I knew why. They were more afraid of offending people than offending God."

Rusty turned and walked back to where I was standing. "If we can't sing and testify to the glory of Jesus, then I don't want any part of it. If we can't live pure and holy for Jesus, then I don't want to be part of the group." He paused, then looked me straight in the eye. "But I think the Lord wants us to use the best modern methods available to communicate His message. And that means getting a better PA system."

That made sense. The next day Rusty and Sam started their search for better equipment, and even though we didn't have the money they finally came up with three microphones (to replace our one mike), a fifty-watt amplifier, and two speakers. The total cost was two hundred fifty dollars, and we thought we had the best sound system in the world.

Rusty still wasn't satisfied. Two weeks later he dropped by the house. Vestel fixed him a cup of coffee and we sat at the table talking. "Howard, we've got to make a record."

"Now wait a minute, Rusty," I said trying to keep from choking, "I went along with you on the sound equipment, but we can't make a record."

"Sure we can," he said. "Our style of music will sell." Rusty had gotten up from the table and was pacing back and forth in front of the kitchen door.

Vestel stuck her head through the door and asked, "Who'll record us?"

"Well, I don't know," Rusty answered. "But that's where the money is. We've got to have something to help us. We can't make it like this."

"Talk to Sam," I said. "If he agrees, then see what you can do."

The next day Rusty drove to Nashville to try to line us up with a recording company. Every place he went we were turned down. He tried established companies like Heartwarming, Songs of Faith, even his old buddy John T. Benson. All shook their heads and said we were too much of a risk.

In a last ditch effort Rusty contacted Russell Sims who had a small business that was about to go on the rocks. "Russell, you don't know this group but we want to make a record. We feel like we can make you some money out of it because one day the Happy Goodmans are really going places in gospel music."

Russell shook his head. "Rusty, I'm just as broke as you are. In fact, I'm just about to go out of business. If you can come up with six hundred dollars cash to pay the union musicians, I might be able to work out something with you. If not, then forget it."

It was Friday night when Rusty came by the house to tell us the bad news. Sam was sitting in the living room, slumped down in a big old easy chair. He spoke up. "Vestel, do you reckon we could borrow six hundred dollars from Mrs. Troop?"

Vestel looked at Sam and grinned. "Let's go talk to her."

Saturday morning Daisy Troop loaned us the money, and we signed a contract Monday to cut our first record with Sims Records. The title: "I'm Too Near Home."

"It will take another month to get the record ready," Russell told us after we had made the tape in the studio. "We've got to produce the master, get the album jackets ready, and then press the records."

In the meantime we were to sing on a Friday night at a wide spot in the road called Pall Mall, Tennessee. When we arrived, there were only five people present. After waiting around for half an hour and no one else showed up, Rusty said, "Howard, Sam, tell you what let's do. Tonight's the night of the all-night singing in Nashville. Let's give these folks their money back and drive over there and see if Wally Fowler will let us on the program."

Sam looked over at me and shrugged his shoulders. "Sounds good. Let's go."

We pulled up in front of Ryman Auditorium, the home of the Grand Old Opry, at 10:00 P.M. The auditorium was packed with more than three thousand happy, excited people.

Wally Fowler greeted us like we were long lost brothers. He hadn't heard the group since the girls had left and we had started back with the boys and Vestel.

"Howard, I want you all to sing a couple of numbers for us. You know we go on the air at 11:00 P.M. for an hour over WSM. However, I can put you on at 10:45 and you can sing for fifteen minutes before we let our regulars come on for the broadcast."

We hit the stage at 10:45. Some of the old fans hadn't seen us in years and were totally unprepared for the new sound of the Happy Goodmans. We came on strong singing "Born to Serve the Lord." They almost tore the building down with their applause. Rusty had just written "I Wouldn't Take Nothing for My Journey Now." Even though he was under contract with Jimmy Davis to have it published, we had been singing it on our TV show. We did it for our second number, and I thought the people were going to tear down the stage with their clapping and shouting.

They wouldn't let us quit. By now it was 11:00 P.M. and I cast a worried glance over at Wally in the wings. He just grinned and motioned for us to go ahead. The fans weren't going to let us quit anyway and kept shouting for more encores. We were on stage until 11:30, and even then we had to turn our backs on the clamoring crowd in order to leave.

Wally met us backstage. "That was fantastic," he said excitedly. "Here's seventy-five dollars, and we want you folks back next month at the same time."

Vestel said, "Wally, we hadn't expected any pay. We're just thankful for the chance to sing."

"Well, if you come back next month I'll give you one hundred fifty dollars," he said enthusiastically. "Those folks out there sure enjoyed the Goodmans tonight."

The next "first Friday" we were back in Ryman Auditorium.

Russell Sims met us and brought the first shipment of records. That night we were on program with the singers from the Gospel Singing Caravan, which was the hottest thing in the country at the time. The program included such groups as the Prophets, the LeFevres, the Blue Ridge Quartet, the Johnson Sisters, the Blackwood Brothers, the Statesmen Quartet, and the Sego Brothers. We didn't even have a place to set up our record table (in fact, we didn't even have a table). So during the intermission we sold our records off the apron of the stage. They went like hotcakes. The people trampled over each other getting to them. The other singing groups all had specials on their records—two for five dollars or three for ten dollars. We only had one album and sold it for the full price—four dollars. That night we not only recovered our six hundred dollars but came away with a nice profit.

We became regulars on the Nashville program and were soon participating in the big Atlanta singings. Invitations were coming in from all over the South—far more than we could accept. For the first time in our lives we were making enough money to live on. It was a satisfying feeling.

Our growing popularity, accompanied with invitations to sing across the nation, soon convinced us we needed a bus. Rusty said he knew where we could get one, so I went with him to look at it. It was in Dallas, Texas, and was an old Trailways bus, a 1947 GMC model 3703. The "37" meant it was supposed to carry that many passengers, and the "03" meant it wasn't air-conditioned.

"Rusty," I said walking around the old bus in the parking lot and kicking at the tires, "I can just see us broke down with this old junker."

However, I listened to Rusty's urgings, and we were soon the owners of a 1947, GMC model 3703 bus. Almost immediately I felt Rusty had led us over the precipice of frustration into the pit of financial despair.

Our first need was for a driver. One person came to mind— Bobby. Not a day had passed that we hadn't prayed for Bobby. He had moved to Shreveport after leaving Evansville and worked with a rock-'n'-roll band in nightclubs. He had made a mess of his life and was finally drafted into the service. Following his discharge he went to work as a truck driver in Dallas. We invited him to come up and look over the bus and talk the situation over with us.

It was a hot July afternoon when Bobby pulled into the parking lot beside the church on Grapevine Road. After greeting us he stood around the churchyard watching Rusty and Sam rip out the back seats of the bus. They were building partitions for three small bedrooms, complete with bunks and closets. Bobby stood around for a long time, looking. Finally he walked up to Sam who was kneeling in the grass, hammering braces into position to make a partition.

"You know, Sam, if you fellows won't make me do anything else, and will leave me free so I can do some fishing, hunting, and work on my old junk cars, I'll move up here and drive this old bus for you."

Sam looked up, the sweat running off his face, and smelled the aroma of Vestel's country ham that drifted out of the nearby parsonage. "I don't reckon Vestel's home cooking helped influence your decision, did it?"

Bobby wrinkled his forehead and rubbed the back of his neck. "Well, that may have helped 'flavor' it a little bit."

Bobby returned to Dallas to pick up his things, and two weeks later he was installed as the official driver of the Goodman family bus. None of us ever dreamed that in the future we would be able to hire a full-time driver and that Bobby would join our musical group as our bass player and a soloist.

It was a bitter cold night in February when the bus first broke down—on the highway outside Montgomery at midnight. After trying unsuccessfully to get it started again, Bobby walked a mile to a phone booth and called a wrecker. They towed us into Montgomery, and we sat around half a day while they put it back into running condition.

A week later we were traveling the same road. It was Saturday night and we had just finished a concert and were heading home.

Rusty had just taken over the wheel so Bobby could go back and lie down. Bobby grinned and pointed down the dark highway. "Rusty, just as we crest that hill up yonder, sit down on the horn. It's right there we broke down, and I almost froze to death walking to a phone."

Rusty laughed and started to hit the horn, but before he could the engine began to sputter and cough. "Oh, no," Bobby shouted as the engine died and Rusty guided the bus to the shoulder of the road.

"I've got to get back to Madisonville in time for church in the morning," I told the group. "I promised the Lord when we started singing full time that if at all possible I would be in my pulpit on Sunday morning and evening and on Wednesday night—even though we're not drawing any salary from the church anymore. I think this old bus has got a devil anyway, and I'm getting off."

"How in the world do you think you're going to get to Madisonville this time of night?" Sam asked.

"The Couriers are right behind us in their old bus. Me and Vestel can hitch a ride with them into Montgomery airport and catch the late plane into Nashville. I'll call someone to meet us, and we'll be home for church in the morning."

"Well, I'm going too," said Sam.

"Me, too," said Rusty.

"That means I get stuck with the bus again."

"You're the driver," Sam laughed as he patted Bobby on the back.

"That means I've gotta walk back up that steep hill in this freezing wind and call the wrecker again," Bobby mumbled. "I promised myself that when I got out of the army I'd never be caught standing outside in the cold any more. Now I'm saying to myself, 'Self, I think you done made the wrong move again.' "

We piled aboard the Couriers' bus, and they drove us to Montgomery while Bobby waited for the wrecker. When he got out to help the mechanic hitch the tow chain to the bumper, the big hook on the end of the chain swung loose and clunked Bobby in the head above his eye, splitting his eyebrow right down the middle.

The mechanic had some old gauze in the cab of the truck, and he wrapped Bobby's head the best he could. The blood continued to ooze through, however, and he looked like a pirate that had been in a fight with Blackbeard and lost.

After hooking the bus to the wrecker they pulled it into the outskirts of Montgomery. At dawn they approached a roadside cafe and Bobby said, "Man, I gotta have some coffee."

They pulled up in front of the restaurant and Bobby stumbled out of the wrecker, his head wrapped in the blood-soaked bandage. The old bus, with the big HAPPY GOODMAN FAMILY sign on the side, was still hitched to the wrecker. Suddenly a woman came bursting out the cafe door, screaming and holding her hands in the air. "Oh Lordy," she screamed, "the Goodmans has been wiped out."

It took Bobby almost a month to stop laughing, but at least it pointed out that we were becoming well known across the South.

It also pointed out something else. We were going to have to get a new bus or get out of the singing business. We had been saving our money in order to make a ten-thousand-dollar down payment on a new Silver Eagle from Trailways. However, we had also made two more records with Sims and now someone else was getting ready to buy him out. In order to protect our investment we had to buy back our three masters—using eight thousand of the ten thousand we had saved for the new bus. Our hopes of getting reliable transportation almost faded away.

The fourth time we broke down it caused us to miss our Sunday church service. This was more than Vestel could take, and that Sunday morning, sitting outside the old garage in Tennessee waiting for the mechanic to show up, Vestel went back to her bunk and knelt on the floor. "Lord," she prayed, "I'm fixing to put out another fleece. Either we're in the wrong business or we've been asking amiss in our prayers. Whatever it is, Lord, I don't think you intend for us to be sitting out here on Sunday morning when we should be in church. Therefore Lord, if you want us to stay in the singing business, I'm asking you to give us eight thousand dollars no later than Monday night so we can buy a new bus. If we don't get it by then, I'll take that as a sign you want us out of the singing business."

It was a bold prayer and when she related the contents to us our faith faltered. Not only were the Goodmans receiving glowing recognition wherever we sang, but Vestel had been proclaimed the "Queen of Gospel Music." Yet, if the Lord wanted us to give all this up we were willing to submit to His will.

Monday morning I received a phone call from Marvin Norcross at Word Records in Waco, Texas. "Howard, we understand that the Goodmans are looking for a recording company. Word Records is prepared to offer you eight thousand dollars if you will sign with us."

Talk about shouting! Mr. Norcross must have thought he was plugged into Yankee Stadium the day the Yanks won the pennant. That afternoon we called Trailways and placed our order for a brand new, double-decker Silver Eagle—the first such bus ever to be sold to a gospel singing group. It was to be custom made in their factory in Belgium and would cost almost fifty-five thousand dollars when complete.

It was a big day (or rather night) when Bobby, Rusty, and Sam flew to New Orleans to pick up the bus. Taking their flashlights they walked the pier until they spotted the huge silver and maroon bus that had been unloaded with the other Trailways buses from Belgium. The big sign stood out in the beams of their flashlights: THE HAPPY GOODMAN FAMILY. There was a long moment of silence, broken only by the sound of the waves lapping against the pier and the lonely clanging of a buoy bell in the harbor. Each boy had his own memories . . . a mule-drawn wagon . . . a Model-T Ford filled with happy Goodman kids . . . a Pepto-Bismol pink Chrysler limousine that was returned to the factory. Sam walked over to the shiny new bus which was to be our home-away-from-home and gently rubbed his fingers against the stainless steel exterior. "Can this really be ours?" he said shaking his head. "Has this really happened to the Happy Goodmans?"

Rusty slid his hand along the big sign that carried our name.

"Yes, it's ours. But first of all it's God's. Had it not been for Him, where would we be?"

These thoughts stayed with Rusty, and a year later he sat down at the organ and wrote what was to become one of his finest compositions.

> Just suppose God searched through Heaven,
> He couldn't find one willing to be;
> The supreme sacrifice that was needed,
> That would buy eternal life for you and me.
>
> Oh! Had it not been for a place called Mount Calv'ry,
> Had it not been for the old rugged cross;
> Had it not been for a Man called Jesus,
> Then forever my soul would be lost.

Chapter Eighteen

There's nothing in the world that'll ever take the place of God's
*   love.*
Silver and gold could never buy His love from above.
When my soul needs healin' and I begin to feelin' His pow'r,
I can say "thank the Lord, I wouldn't take nothing for my
*   journey now."*

             —RUSTY GOODMAN

Ernie Maxwell joined us in 1967 as our lead guitarist. Ernie
and Jo Ellen became members of the Goodman family. The lead
guitar not only handles the introductions but also fills between
verses and phrases. The guitarists we had before tried to make us
sing for them, rather than playing for us. But as an artist with
the guitar, Ernie knew just how much to leave out as well as how
much to put in. With Bobby playing bass and Rusty playing
rhythm, our instrumental section was about complete.

The following year, at the age of sixteen, Ricky joined us on
the drums. His expert touch gave the Happy Goodmans the
biggest, fullest, and most complete sound in contemporary gospel
music. We had been on a syndicated TV program, "The Gospel
Singing Jubilee," for two years and our programs were purchased
and run over more than one hundred television stations all over
the nation on a weekly basis. Besides our three earlier records,
we cut six more for Word's Canaan Records division, and the
demand continued to grow for more. Thus it seemed an almost
foregone conclusion that when the National Academy of Recording Arts and Sciences presented their Grammy Award for the best

gospel performance of 1968, it would go to the Happy Goodman Family. Dressed in tuxedos we stood on the stage in Nashville with such greats as Johnny Cash and June Carter to receive the academy's award as America's Number One Gospel Singers—the only straight gospel group ever to receive the coveted award.

However, even in the midst of this success as we rode the crest of the wave of fame, there were still times of depression. I guess it's natural, after having been poor all our lives, to be afraid that the bubble of success might burst and leave us floundering. Yet, as we continued to walk in the light of God's grace we found His power always sufficient.

It was the year before that Rusty fell into one of those moods of depression. Every time I saw him he looked like he wanted to cry. Vestel and I prayed with and for him, but nothing seemed to help him.

We had driven to Nashville to tape some TV shows. Rusty had a separate room and all that first night Vestel and I prayed for him. The next morning we were sitting at the breakfast table in the coffee shop when Rusty walked in. Sitting down at the table he looked at Vestel and said, "Do you want to hear something the Lord gave me early this morning?"

Vestel looked up at him and said, "Sure, Rusty. What is it?"

Rusty pulled out an old scrap of paper and started singing, right there in the coffee shop. As he sang, big tears of joy rolled down his face. Completely unaware of anyone around us in the coffee shop, Vestel and I both broke into tears. Rusty lifted his arms over his head and his voice filled the coffee shop as he sang his newly composed song.

> Who am I that a king would bleed and die for?
> Who am I that He would pray, "not my will thine" for?
> The answer I may never know;
> Why He ever loved me so;
> That to an old rugged cross He'd go
> For who am I?
>
> When I'm reminded of His words, I'll leave thee never,
> Just be true I'll give to you a life forever . . .

I wonder what I could have done to deserve God's only Son;
Fight my battles till they're won,
Who am I?

He finished singing and a holy hush fell over the coffee shop.
Even the waitresses were standing with heads bowed. Vestel
reached up and wiped the tears from her cheeks and said, "Rusty,
you ought to go back up to your room and ask God for another
valley. You'd never got that song had you stayed on the moun-
taintop. The richest soil is always down in the valley."

I guess it's because we've spent so much time in the valley that
we've seen so much of the fruit of the Spirit. In September of 1967
we moved into our new $150,000 church building. Brother E. W.
Jackson gave us the property and we sold bonds (of which the
Goodman family bought forty thousand dollars worth) to
finance the building construction. However, the larger building
was a necessity. Not only were we reaching more of the Madisonville people in our ministry, but every Sunday scores of people
were driving for hundreds of miles to attend our services.

The Goodman family bought the old church property. We
fixed a place in the back so mama could park her trailer and be
near our house at the same time. We remodeled the basement
of the old church offices, while upstairs in the auditorium we
installed a sophisticated recording studio with some of the finest
equipment in the nation. None of us had forgotten what it was
like to try to find a studio that would record "poor folks." Just as
the church was built to minister to the poor, so it was with the
recording studio. We hadn't forgotten—and we never will—that
God's work always comes first.

On his tenth wedding anniversary Sam did something he had
wanted to do ever since he had been married—he brought home
a beautiful diamond ring and slipped it on Barbara's finger.

About three weeks later he came in late one afternoon and
Barbara asked him to come in the kitchen.

"Sit down, honey," she said. "Now before I say anything else

I want you to know I love you more than any person in all this
world."

Sam said, "I believe that."

"I don't know of anything I ever wanted more than a diamond
ring. When I was a little girl, having to wear dresses made out
of feed bags in order to go to school, I thought the most wonderful thing in all the world would be to have a diamond ring. But
I feel like you and me could do more for the church if you'd give
this ring back. Instead of making payments on it, we could give
the money to God."

She pulled the expensive ring from her finger and put it in
her husband's hand. Sam looked at it, glittering in his palm, then
looked up at the sparkling eyes of his beautiful wife. Pulling her
close to him he buried his face in the folds of her skirt and wept.

The next morning Sam returned the ring to Sonny Bryant at
the jewelry store. After hearing the story the jeweler credited his
account with the full amount he had already paid on the ring.

Strange, perhaps . . . but that's the way God has always dealt
with us Goodmans. And that's the way we respond to Him.

I guess our brother Rusty has put it into song for all of us.

> I started out trav'lin for the Lord many years ago.
> I've had a lotta heartache, met a lotta grief and woe.
> And when I would stumble, then I would humble down,
> And there I would say I wouldn't take nothin' for my journey
>   now.

> Well, I wouldn't take nothin' for my journey now,
> I've gotta make it to Heav'n somehow
> Though the Devil tempts me and tries to turn me around;
> He offered everything that's got a name
> All the wealth I want and worldly fame;
> If I could, still I wouldn't take nothin' for my journey now.